D0786246

Templado
A Star at Liberty

Templado
A Star at Liberty

Lætitia **BOULIN-NÉEL**

Frédéric **PIGNON**

Magali **DELGADO**

Photographs

Frédéric **CHÉHU**

Hervé **JULLIAN**

Thierry **SÉGARD**

Translated from the French by

Graham **BUSHNELL**

Éditions Cavalia

Lætitia Boulin-Néel is a journalist with *Cheval Pratique* magazine.

Thierry Segard is a photographer for *Cheval Pratique*.

Published by arrangement with *Templado, la star en liberté* ©Éditions Belin-Paris-2002

Le code de la propriété intellectuelle n'autorise que «les copies ou reproductions strictement réservées à l'usage privé du copiste et non destinées à une utilisation collective» [article L. 122-5]; il autorise également les courtes citations effectuées dans un but d'exemple ou d'illustration. En revanche «toute représentation ou reproduction intégrale ou partielle, sans le consentement de l'auteur ou de ses ayants droit ou ayants cause, est illicite» [article L. 122-4]. La loi 95-4 du 3 janvier 1994 a confié au C.F.C. (Centre français de l'exploitation du droit de copie, 20, rue des Grands-Augustins, 75006 Paris), l'exclusivité de la gestion du droit de reprographie. Toute photocopie d'œuvres protégées, exécutée sans son accord préalable, constitue une contrefaçon sanctionnée par les articles 425 et suivants du Code pénal.

© Éditions Cavalia, 2006

ISBN 2-7011-3822-1

Printed in Canada

Contents

"I hope you will agree that life would be very sad indeed

if there were not, from time to time,

a few brief moments of pure and unexpected joy.

On the bend of a lane near Avignon, a magnificent house comes into view (I find out later that it is a stables), a window opens

and a horse looks out at me,

a vision that might have come straight from an artist's palette.

And time stands still. I had no idea that a horse could be so beautiful, so free.

Never before, in my whole life, have I seen such a sight. Man and horse locked in a silent exchange.

An animal that is happy and fulfilled, who accepts obedience only to the voice or the whisper of his friends Frédéric and Magali.

I am sure that this book will give you an overwhelming desire to make their acquaintance and share this same joy with them."

Introduction

People who know about horses will understand me. To devote a whole book to one single horse is quite a daring thing to do, especially if it includes attributing human feelings to the horse in question! But I can feel his eyes watching my every move – and how can you talk about a horse without giving him a soul? How can you make him come alive without giving him feelings and emotions in human terms that bring him closer to us?

When Frédéric and Magali suggested that I write a tribute to Templado, it took a long time for me to make up my mind. After all, I am just a journalist. I spend my time writing very down-to-earth material designed to help horsemen, give them advice and show them how to conduct their relationships with horses.

To write about one particular horse seemed to me to be a dangerous venture and somewhat beyond my limitations. So why did I take up the challenge?

Probably because this particular horse is not just any old horse and this is the determining factor in making this book what it is.

An even stronger reason is that all five members of the Delgado-Pignon family have put their complete – blind – trust in me. It's one thing to know someone well, as they know me, but quite another for them to give me a free rein... For this, I thank them, as they have opened all the doors for me.

As for Templado, how can I thank him? He has freed me from the burden of my worries. For he is the one who did all the work. I only had to write down what he dictated. He is a fabulous horse – almost unique. Whether attentive or mocking, bad-tempered or gentle, he is always well-bred and never vulgar. To Frédéric, and only Frédéric, he shows respect, for he has unlimited confidence in him. It was a delight to watch Templado for hours on end – in his stall at home, in liberty training, in performance and in photo sessions. Each new meeting showed me a new facet of his personality, as if he was taking some wicked delight in only revealing a little of himself at a time. In his stall, for example, I was royally snubbed at first. Then he granted me visiting rights, on condition that I was chaperoned by Frédéric. Finally, he accepted me on my own. In the end, I even had the immense privilege of being able to stroke him without getting a well-aimed kick. Templado is charismatic, professional and easy to become attached to, and if you think at any time on reading this homage that I am being excessive, I can assure you that I have in no way betrayed his personality, for this horse is excessive in everything – forever on the move, a complete and complex personality. In a word, he is everything except what his name suggests, for, in Spanish, Templado means temperate!

Laetitia Boulin-Néel

Prologue

"All this fuss made about him, and he'll never know anything about it," was what I found myself saying one day to Frédéric Pignon, when we needed more photos than just the ones from the various shows and had to schedule several photo sessions. "Don't worry about him. I'll go and read him the book by candlelight one evening," said Frédéric, laughing.

■ From left to right, Frédéric and Dao, Magali and Bandolero, Estelle and Guisot, Joëlle and Dueno, Pierre and Damao.

■ Three good friends relaxing.

Frédéric is devoted to horses, like no one else. If I had to make a list of people who really knew horses, I would put him at the top, followed by all the Delgado in-laws.

This is a family who share the same consuming passion and have managed the feat of setting up the finest stock farm of Lusitanian horses in France over the last thirty years. These are the horses that Estelle, Magali and Frédéric present in performance. The Delgado horses, now envied by Portuguese and Spanish breeders alike, all have the two "house" stallions in their blood line: Perdigon VI (31 years old) and Zagalotte (21 years old). If you count Magali and Frédéric's show stables and the family stock farm about six miles away, the Delgado-Pignons have more than 120 Lusitanians: mares, foals, young horses, adult males, mature horses, stallions… They all have their own particular story and their own word to say.

So why devote a whole book to just one of them? What is so special about Templado that made Magali and Frédéric so determined to embark on such an ambitious project?

Templado is one of those exceptional horses that leave their mark on your life. He has shaped the lives of five of the Delgado-Pignon family, notably Magali and Frédéric, over the 13 years or so that he has shared their daily lives.

Templado was born at the Delgados' and sold as a one-year-old. Three years later, he came back home, having given his owner more than he bargained for. He was rebellious, fearful, misunderstood, difficult to understand and even dangerous – the result of being locked into a violent resistance to man during his early years.

By patient observation and trial and error, Frédéric and Magali gradually managed to persuade him to come out of his shell. It took five long years for Templado to recognise his unconditional friendship for Frédéric. Five long years of searching, doubting and questioning, which enabled Frédéric and Magali to take a major step forward in their knowledge and understanding of horses. Their philosophy and sensitivity – as much in their approach to a horse's freedom both with a rider in the saddle or in liberty training – is based on what they have learned from Templado over these long years.

Today Frédéric and Magali are fluent speakers of horse language. And the one who taught them the syntax and grammar of this difficult tongue was Templado. It is therefore quite natural that the two pupils should find a way of giving thanks to their master.

Spotlight on Templado

■ Templado, the "dancing horse" in Santo Domingo.

The cossack number has just ended to thunderous applause. The frantic gallop has had the five thousand people around the ring on the edge of their seats, trembling with the pleasurable thrill of apprehension and excitement. Now the horses are racing around in line with their riders doing stunts on their backs: they do headstands, dismount while the horses are moving, get back on, slide under the bellies of their mounts and disappear behind their flanks. Amazing. Then, after taking a shimmering bow, horses and riders exit at full gallop in cossack style. One after another, they disappear, swallowed up by the red curtain that hides the backstage area from the audience.

Everything suddenly goes black and, as if their temperature has been lowered by the pitch black darkness that has followed the wild antics of the stunt riders, the crowd becomes silent. We can only be sure of their presence because of a few exchanged whispers and throats being cleared.

And then the lights go full up on the middle of the ring where a man is now standing, alone. Tall, slim and athletic, he gives a broad, sincere smile, showing how delighted he is to be there. He is dressed in black boots and trousers with a fitted royal blue velvet jacket, embroidered with gold thread. In his hands he holds two slender black sticks of different lengths.

The man is Frédéric Pignon. Many of the audience recognise him immediately when the lights converge on him. Some have even come especially to see him and his partner, Magali Delgado. The music starts, languorous and poetic.

A pale blue follow-spot suddenly picks up what seems to be a streak of white lightning that shoots out from the red curtain, cutting through the air like a rocket.

Is it a vision – a hallucination? The whole audience ripples with a gasp of open-mouthed admiration.

The "rocket" that has just emerged at the speed of light stops suddenly in the middle of the ring. No, this is not Pegasus who has descended from the heavens, but a white horse, as handsome as Apollo and with a seemingly endless mane. He stands there, the centre of attention, in a pose that is totally natural, as if to say, "I am here, lord of all I survey." And five thousand people are bowled over by such grace, power and presence.

Then, half rearing up, he turns his back on them and takes off again. His mane, which had fallen in a rippling cascade down to the ground, suddenly rises up like a fountain and becomes a spray of pink, blue and white light. The audience tries to absorb these breathtakingly beautiful images, unable to see the horse clearly, yet overwhelmed by the magic of this superb, majestic animal.

Once again, the dancing horse stands still for a moment and shows off his magnificent physique. Like a lion, Templado nonchalantly basks in the sun of the spotlights. Then something disturbs him and the lion awakes, bounding in all directions, springing about like a youngster. His thick mane envelops him, its white strands washing over his back and head. He goes straight to his prey at full tilt. Ears laid back, nostrils dilated, eyes bright with joy, he bounds towards it then rears up to make it

■ Two brothers with contrasting characters but a family resemblance: Templado and Fasto.

cower in awe. Then, straight as a die, he holds the pose proudly, folding his knees in as if to box himself, and sparing his victim from a certain death. With a light, elegant movement, he comes down to earth from his great height, stands right in front of the thing that caused him so much fury and changes from an angry lion into a harmless sheep. As if vanquished in battle, he lies down gently, then slowly raises himself up and sits down obediently. His long orderly mane covers his shoulders. He looks calm and peaceful, but there is a mocking, knowing look in his eye. The arrogant Templado has lowered his guard and avowed that he has a weak spot for this "prey" who is, in fact, his partner.

It is then that the crowd again registers the presence of Frédéric Pignon. The trick has worked, for they had forgotten he was there. With one hand, he gently strokes the horse's muzzle while acknowledging the audience with the other. And still that smile… The audience are so moved that they go silent, not daring to disturb such fairytale magic.

But the mask has fallen and the audience can now delight in watching the two companions at play. Frédéric signals to Templado to get up. The horse looks at him and slowly rises. With studied vigour, he shakes his whole body and the white mane flies up, raising the dust.

Frédéric takes off at top speed, running as fast as he can. Templado lets him go, then he bends his head, tosses his mane and whips his tail. Without warning, he takes up the chase and easily catches Frédéric in a few strides. He pretends to bite his master, to remind him that no one escapes from Templado with impunity. At first it seems that the horse will not budge, and then he nonchalantly releases Frédéric. Then he follows Frédéric, never overtaking him but keeping up with him all the time and dogging every step. They break into a trot and Templado shows himself at full stretch, displaying all the muscles of his athletic body.

Suddenly Frédéric stops and, as if by magic, his accomplice imitates him. They both move back together. The horse behaves as if Frédéric were the star and he were his greatest fan. To prove it, Templado bows before him.

You can feel the tension in the audience. They want to express their admiration, respect and joy but they don't have time because the curtain opens and a second white horse enters at a trot. Looking as proud as a peacock, he comes to join his brother, who is eight years his senior. The audience wonders at the resemblance and at the achievement of bringing two such powerful stallions together, and both as free as air. The handsome young brother, Fasto, is intimidated by being next to such a star, even though it is his big brother. Naturally, he takes his cue

■ Paris Bercy, 2002: from left to right, Templado, Amoroso and Fasto.

from him but, wary of getting in the way of any show of temperament from this capricious lion, he finds comfort next to Frédéric, whose eyes do not leave him. Templado plays with his young brother and, nosing him gently, puts him in his place. Each in his own way, the two brothers compete for the favours of their master. Fasto obeys without question. Templado negotiates in order to get the attention he demands: before doing anything that is asked of him, he makes sure that everyone realises that it is his own choice to do so. Their dance begins: a waltz around Frédéric who directs the ballet with his two sticks. In a final movement, Templado and Fasto plunge into a bow and flood the ground with their silken manes.

At this precise moment, when the number ends, the audience is speechless, moved to a silent, lump-in-the-throat emotion by such grace. And then the silence is broken. Bravos ring out and there is thunderous applause. Some people rise from their seats and the rest of the audience, without realising what they are doing, follow the movement and get to their feet. A total triumph.

As the audience leave their seats, one spectator in particular is filled with emotion. This is the fourth time he has come under the spell of Templado and each time the feeling is just as overwhelming. Now, as an unconditional fan, he simply has to meet this astonishing horse.

He plucks up the courage to go backstage and, like a child with stagefright, stammers a few banal remarks to Frédéric and Magali. Fully aware of how ridiculous he must appear, he nevertheless goes so far as to ask the impossible. Could he come to their home – at a time when it's convenient, of course – to say hello to the star and steal a few strands of his magical mane by way of an autograph?

He receives a frank, friendly and generous reply. He will be most welcome, naturally, if it can be arranged. The fan could not wish for anything more and returns home to plan his forthcoming trip…

■ Templado at the International Paris-Bercy show-jumping event, in front of 15,000 spectators.

2

A very discreet hero

■ A long-standing relationship between Magali and Dao, the other star of the stables.
Right-hand page
■ Templado does his daily jogging.

Going to see Templado in his own home can be a bit bewildering for the first-time visitor. Looking at the twenty-two occupants of the stables that belong to Magali and Frédéric, he has a lot of trouble identifying the sublime, light-footed actor that he has come to see, for all these white Lusitanians have the same elegance. It is as if they have conspired to hide the star from curious eyes and pushy paparazzi.

The visitor is aware of the honour bestowed on him and hurries impatiently towards the stalls in the hope of finding the streaming mane that enfolds the capricious star in mystery.

Having taken only a few steps inside the stables, he is stopped dead in his tracks by a pair of eyes which render him speechless. They belong to Dao. Dao from Courennes is to Magali what Templado is to Frédéric – an inseparable companion both for shows and dressage competitions.

As if drawn by a magnet by the sight of such power in repose, the visitor advances very slowly, wary of disturbing the majestic pose of the white stallion. Dao stands there imperturbably, like an 18th century engraving or bronze statue, his fine, proud, well-bred, elegant head framed by the window of his stall. His silky, luminous coat and mane contrast with the depth of his dark, proud eyes. Could this be the most beautiful horse in the world? When the visitor sees him for the first time, there can be no doubt. Entranced, he goes towards the god-like animal. He puts out a hand tentatively to stroke the horse's muzzle and looks into the stall, almost embarrassed by his daring. This could be high treason. But his daring is rewarded. With the graciousness of those who know themselves to be beautiful, Dao retains his haughty pose in order to be admired. This proud, serene majesty is beauty in its raw state – perfection of line, curve, shape and volume.

The visitor is hesitant to move away but does so and tries to get a grip on himself as he advances into the first stable,

Guisot

Fasto

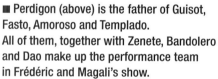

■ Perdigon (above) is the father of Guisot, Fasto, Amoroso and Templado.
All of them, together with Zenete, Bandolero and Dao make up the performance team in Frédéric and Magali's show.

passing in front of Templado without even realising it. The 'Lord of the Manor' is more amused than vexed at being ignored in this way and witnesses the scene quietly from his stall, looking thoughtful. Anyone who knows him can see a slightly disdainful look in his eyes – tinted with a dash of humour – directed as much at the stranger as at Dao. Templado is extremely possessive and reserves his favours exclusively for his favourite, Frédéric. He cares nothing for using his charm on just any old admirer. Sure of his own starring role and brilliance in performance, he sees no point in playing the star at home in the stables. He leaves that to his younger and vainer companions.

The visitor looks for the unending mane with its deceptive transparency under the stream of braids. He then notices Bandolero, tender and cream-coloured, with his bright blue eyes and pink nostrils. Then he caresses wicked Fasto, gasps in admiration at Guisot, the brown bay so in love with his own colour, politely admires faithful Zenete, greets old Amoroso and steps back when faced by the gigantic Famoso.

Still no Templado? Maybe he's in another stable? Strange, when this one houses all the stars of the show... Or could it be that modest horse over there, hidden away at the back of his stall, limply standing there with his head down? The visitor can hardly believe it. He tries to conjure up the images engraved in his memory of the magical brilliance of that unique horse. He compares them with this very ordinary animal he sees before him and, by superimposing the images on the reality, is

A well-bred

Templado was born on 11th June 1985 in one of the stalls of the Delgado stables in Courennes, ten miles north of Apt in south-eastern France. His father, Perdigon VI, deserves a special mention because he is the one responsible for bringing success to the Delgado family.

Pierre and Joëlle Delgado are the sort of people who are avant-garde by nature and they were among the very first to do performances of equestrian shows – the forerunners of all our present-day equestrian artists. In the 60s and 70s they astounded audiences with their riding abilities. Nothing daunted them – from the craziest of stunts to feats of lassoo throwing – either before a live audience or as actors' stand-ins in front of the camera. They were also experienced and talented horse trainers and presented classic *haute école* dressage numbers.

At that time Joëlle and Pierre bred horses on a small scale and in a somewhat haphazard fashion which made breeding a hit-and-miss affair. However, for years they had wanted to set up a high quality Lusitanian stock farm, along the lines of the Portuguese ones, and distance themselves from the amateurish attitude that then prevailed in France with regard to Iberian horses. One day, they decided to take the plunge, sold their farm and started again from scratch. In order to make a clean start, they first had to acquire some good mares and they went to Portugal to buy fifteen or so Andrade mares, or mares with Andrade blood.

They also needed a very good stallion and, determined to get the very best, went in search of the impossibly perfect one.

They wanted a horse that really only existed in wonderland. A white stallion who was proud but gentle, well made, high-stepping but with good locomotion. As a bonus, the stal-

■ What energy: like father, like son!
Perdigon VI, at the age of thirty, playing like a colt with Joëlle.

family

■ Pierre and Joëlle, who brought Templado into the world.

lion had to have a very long mane which almost touched the ground. In short, they were pursuing a dream! After going through every French stud farm with a fine toothcomb, in 1976 they went off to tour Spain where they searched stock farms and stud farms, from the most reputable downwards. Two months later, they were still empty-handed, so they returned to France, very much downhearted.

A few weeks later, a couple of their friends took the same trip with the same objective. They had more luck and discovered Perdigon VI whom they immediately purchased and brought back to France.

"You can't imagine how amazed we were when we saw the horse of our dreams before us; the very one we had spent months and months looking for. Our friends realised what this horse meant to us and handed him over to us to work him. Then, seeing how attached we had become to him, they were kind enough to leave him with us," remembers Pierre Delgado, still moved by their friends' gesture of 25 years ago.

Magali and Estelle, who were only very young at the time, were very much in awe of the new occupant of the stables.

"I couldn't believe it. We – the little Delgados – we had a real Barbie horse in our stables, just like all little girls dream of; a magical horse with a long mane and an all-white coat!" says

■ Perdigon VI and Joëlle,
a 25-year friendship.

Magali. If the sisters love horses so much now it is all because of Perdigon. How could they not when they could ride such a dream come true almost every day? They were so proud when they walked down the street with him and showed off their new friend's beauty to other little girls.

But Perdigon wasn't there just to spoil two little girls. They may have been very pretty but they needed to be shown a little humility. Since he was given the responsibility of introducing them to performing in front of an audience, he had no compunction when it came to putting them in their place in front of a full house. *"When I had to ride Perdigon in a performance, I was so nervous,"* Magali remembers. *"At home, he was as good as gold – a good learner, hardworking, submissive, and he obeyed orders beautifully. But as soon as he got in the ring, he wasn't the same horse. He was proud and loved being admired by the audience. He knew he wouldn't be punished in public and so he took advantage of this and became almost impossible to control. It was terrible. You never knew what trick he was going to play on us..."*

Perdigon was born in 1971 at the Bohorquez stud farm. Brought up in the Spanish manner in his early years, he was used to treatment in which horse psychology played almost no part. At the Delgados', it was quite a different regime, based on the understanding and analysis of equine behaviour, in which the horses were allowed to express themselves within a pre-established framework that had to be respected. Perdigon wasted no time in taking advantage of this wonderful new regime. At home, he knew how to give pleasure by way of thanks, but in performance it was such fun to play, above all when you knew you couldn't be punished!

"Perdigon's sons have all inherited his grace and pride and his taste for charming an audience. They all love to show off and be admired. But not one of them is as undisciplined as he could be in performance. Probably because they have grown up with us in a caring environment," explains Pierre.

His sweet yet teasing nature soon won over the whole family. Spoiled and pampered, he was the boss, the master, the king. But it has to be said that nothing in his behaviour has ever provoked harsh treatment. He has become like his owners – serene, joyous and very professional.

He was also adored by the mares. With his sensitive, gentle temperament, he knew how to gain the favours of all of them, even the youngest. When the herd of females saw him from afar heading for their field, they would let him approach without showing the least hostility. And today, at the advanced age of 31, Perdigon still mounts his mares, held by Pierre Delgado on a simple halter rein. When one knows how risky natural coverings can be, one can only be astonished at his facility when it comes to charming the mares.

Since he was born in Spain, Perdigon VI is registered and recognised as a stallion in the stud book of pure Spanish breeds. Because they wished to breed Lusitanian horses, in 1982 Pierre and Joëlle Delgado presented him before the Portuguese commission of which Fernando Andrade was a member. The commission recognised him – and gave him a very high mark – as a genetically Lusitanian stallion. His offspring are therefore registered in the Lusitanian stud book. In 1988, the French

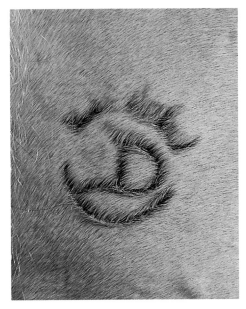

■ The Delgado brand.

National Stud recognised the Lusitanian breed and Perdigon could therefore father fully-documented and approved Lusitanian foals on French territory.

With more than 230 offspring to his account, Perdigon IV has proved to have exceptional genetic qualities. He passes on to his offspring his warm, ebullient and deeply gentle character. He gives them his high-stepping walk, his good locomotion and, as a bonus, he bequeaths them his long thick mane. If one could only mention one of his offspring, let it be the most illustrious: Templado, by far the one who resembles him most closely.

Lequina CN, Templado's mother, is one of the Delgados' horses who can always be depended upon. A good breeder and a good mother, she is one of those affectionate and intelligent mares who instinctively know how to take care of their foals. Joëlle and Pierre had bought her ten years before from a reputable Portuguese stock farm in Val de Santaram on the banks of

■ "Please, tame me!"

the Tagus not far from the Coudelaria Nacional. Lequina arrived in France with the foal that she had given birth to that year. To travel one thousand two hundred and fifty miles in a truck was quite a feat for a foal that was only a few weeks old.

At the age of sixteen, Lequina was at the height of her form when she gave birth to Templado. As usual, she was placed in a foaling stall a few days before the birth. And, as usual, everything went wonderfully well that day – or rather that night, because Templado chose to come into the world in the middle of the night, like most foals. But no matter what the time of day, Joëlle and Pierre never miss a delivery in case of any complication that might arise. They therefore witnessed the foal's first steps and he already seemed to be showing off. *"He looks pro-*

mising, that one," they both thought. *"He's going to be a lively one and a real performer."*

Although he was born rather late in the season, Templado soon made up for this slight handicap and, in a few weeks, caught up with his fifteen brothers and other companions who were slightly older. He played and capered about completely unconcerned by his elders. It has to be said that there was no lack of space for unrestrained gallops: the Delgado stud farm for mares and its 'nursery' covered eight hundred hectares of mountainous pasture land.

The jagged peaks with their caps – *couronnes* in French, meaning mountain caps or crowns and the origin of the name Courennes – also inspired the the Delgado brand that is put on the right thigh of all the horses that are born there. It represents two crowns facing each other, one with prongs, the other without.

An oversensitive foal

Barely weaned, Templado left the Delgado farm at the age of one to go to other Provençal pastures. He did not go alone. His half-brother Terso (by Perdigon), also born during the summer, accompanied him in his new life.

They became part of a herd of horses and lived in a social context that was essential for their future psychological equilibrium. They received a proper 'horse education'. On the other hand, their new owner, even though he was very attached to them, could not unfortunately give them enough time to make strong attachments themselves.

But why was it that Terso seemed to have understood and accepted what was expected of him? And why did Templado revolt?

It would seem that Templado was a hypersensitive horse, much more so than his brother. He needed more communication, contact, touching, the voice, words… in other words he needed the agreeable feeling of having a friendly relationship that would induce him to accept man into his environment. For no apparent reason other than his own extreme sensitivity, he had the impression that he was under attack, which put him in a blind panic. Whenever he saw a man arriving in his field, Templado would run as far away as possible. He refused any human contact and, immuring himself in his fears and anxieties, withdrew into himself. Whenever he emerged from his silence, it was only to respond violently to man's demands. He showed resistance to everything and everything annoyed him.

His owner realised that he had better say goodbye to both Templado and his brother, who therefore returned to their place of birth. They were four years old and were still colts and yet Templado already had a history of revolt behind him…

■ An inconclusive attempt…

Right-hand page
■ Let's try using play.

A deafening return

"The day Templado returned," Magali remembers, "he was really in a pitiful state. His owner could not get near him, there were great lumps of dried mud clinging to his tail and the more he spun round to try and get rid of them, the harder they hit his body; and the harder they hit him, the angrier he became. Spinning around in his stall like a mad thing, his tail banging against the walls of the stall, Templado went mad – maddened by the weight of

his tail, maddened by the noise it made against the walls, maddened with anger at not being able to do anything about it. In a panic, he ended up by hitting out violently with his hind legs, so violently that one leg smashed through the low wall of the stall and got trapped there. He struggled with all his strength to free himself and did some serious damage to his shank where the scar still remains.

"We couldn't get into the stall to get the lumps of dried mud off. It was too risky. The only way out was to pass his tail over the top of the wall and break off the lumps with a hammer! Not an easy thing to do especially since he didn't like being held and had a holy terror of the hammer. As for tending to his injury, I can't tell you how difficult that was!"

Hello there, it's me, I'm back! Despite this noisy return to the Delgado stables, Templado didn't frighten the family that much. Ever since they had set up the farm, they had had to deal with other reticent, wild or misunderstood horses. Other colts before him had come back to the Delgados to be 'rehabilitated' after having had problems elsewhere. It must be said that the incredible beauty of these foals had incited a number of buyers to purchase them too young and when they didn't have the ability to deal with stallions. They found the horses aggressive and beyond control and returned them to be worked by the Delgados. Therefore, Templado came back home with his problems without it being a problem for the family. They knew he was sensitive, vulnerable and fearful and they put up with it. "We never considered him as anything special. No one ever tried to analyse all his psychological problems. He had his worries, just as we had ours." The family thought that he would end up by finding his equilibrium, just like the other horses, through good treatment and understanding.

He was Pierrot's mount and he even took him for rides, without a second thought. The horse was delicate, that was for sure, and nothing could be demanded of him. But as long as he was just taken for a trot outside, he showed no reticence.

If he put any pressure on him, asked him to do more or to work in the outdoor school, Pierrot realised straight away that it would be no easy matter to train him. Templado would have sudden fits of anger, try and get the bit out of his mouth, toss his head violently, push against the leg, refuse to give in, throw up his forelegs and prance. There was no evil intent in his movements, just the expression of complete revolt. No, he would not give in to man; no, he would not submit any more without good reason and without explanation.

At that time, Magali had just lost a horse who was very dear to her – Tenerio. The death of this horse, in whom she had placed so much hope for a future in *haute école* dressage, made her deeply sad. Pierrot therefore gave her Templado who was the same age. Reluctantly, Magali tried in turn to ride Templado, with exactly the same result. The horse put up resistance as soon as one began to use any insistance. *"We often worked with delicate, sensitive or complicated horses,"* Magali explains. *"With patience, understanding and hard work we always managed to make them do what we wanted. No matter how long it took, they always ended by showing themselves willing to comply. With Templado, there was no progression, only resistance. As soon as we used the rein, he would veer to the side. We had the impression that he could not stand the weight of a rider or the bit in his mouth. Therefore, we thought we'd made a big mistake somewhere and that all his problems were physical. We had him examined by a horse osteopath and a horse dentist, but they couldn't find anything wrong. Anyway, I had given up because Templado didn't have the walk or the look of Tenerio and would never give me the results I could have obtained with my own horse. There simply was no point in annoying him with outdoor schooling any more."*

Templado, with his markedly Spanish roots, may not have been a beauty in the academic sense but he looked positively majestic. It seemed obvious that he would look wonderful in performance. But no one ever dreamed of it at the time because the Delgados never forced a horse to do anything. Their philosophy forbade it. So, Templado was in revolt; Templado was afraid. In that case, they would take the time – all the time in the world if necessary – to get his confidence back and make him want to communicate with humans. If he didn't earn his own living, others would earn it for him. What mattered was not his profitability but his own well-being.

There was no precise idea about his future career, so no one from the family would battle with him. When if ever he decided he wanted to work, so much the better. If not, no one was going to insist.

Anyway, even approaching him was a challenge. He was a rebel through and through and anyone who came near him would have to face up to his independence and mistrust. He would refuse to be held and would turn around in his stall, snorting, with his nostrils dilated. A wall of anxiety made him unwilling to communicate in any way, even with the other horses. With them, he became shy and he would huddle up against the walls so as not to be seen.

After months without any progress being made, the family realised the truth of the matter. Any other horse would have come to reason. The proof was that his brother, Terso, who

38

Below
■ One of the rare appearances of Frédéric riding Templado, second from the left.

had returned to the stables with him, found his feet much more easily. So what made Templado so different? It was probably a hypersensitivity so strong that, for example, he had to be forwarned before accepting the slightest caress.

Noisy parades

The equestrian events held at places such as Nimes, St-Rémi-de-Provence and Saintes-Maries-de-la-Mer are etched indelibly on the memories of the whole family.

At the beginning of the 90s, when Templado came back to the stables, the Delgado family took part in all the equestrian parades of the region. They were still fairly unknown and, for them, it was a the best means of showing off the products of their stud farm to a large audience and to the professionals who attended the events. The aim was to show the horses that would represent the Delgados to their best advantage. Despite his rebellious nature, Templado was one of these and he too had to parade. It was an opportunity for him to get used to the noise and to

people, and to dive into the mad chaos of Mediterranean festivities. It would be a good initiation if one distant day he was ever to perform in public.

The road to hell is paved with good intentions… After a few attempts, the five members of the family decided, by common agreement, to put an end to Templado's career on the street. *"We would hold his mane and wait for something to happen,"* says Magali. *"The other horses, the music, the din – all that had no effect on him at all. He was furious at being ridden. He could stand there for a quarter of an hour in the same place, not wanting to go forward, resisting with all his strength. He wasn't trying to get rid of us, he was just showing his violent exasperation!"*

4

A rebel through and through

In 1991, when Frédéric and Magali decided to set up a performance stable alongside the stock farm, they moved away from the family fold and went to Tavel, in the Gard region. Tavel turned out to be good choice, being well located both for the horse business as well as a base from which to travel to performances. When they moved, Templado went with them, along with the rest of the horses.

Up to now, every attempt to communicate with Templado had ended in failure because he would systematically put up a wall between them, and nothing could break it down. He had a deep mistrust of everything that emanated from human beings. As soon as the slightest thing upset him, he would dig his heels in and nothing could make him amenable or change his mind. Everything became a subject of conflict. There would have been conflicts every day if Frédéric and Magali had tried to tackle the problem by force. But, rather than take the bull by the horns, they decided to leave Templado alone, which meant that nothing really constructive was achieved.

"If we leave him alone, he'll soon tire of all this and will end up breaking down the barriers of his own accord," thought Frédéric. But this wasn't to be. Time passed and nothing changed. If he was on the lungeing rein and the slightest move seemed suspicious, he could explode and break the rein in one movement, without any warning. Frédéric therefore tried liberty training, but this was even worse. Templado showed the full extent of his uncontrollable fears.

"We let him out in the outdoor school to see how he would behave. I thought I would never get him back again," says Frédéric. *"He would have done anything, even killed himself, rather than be caught again. I was the embodiment of everything that had to be escaped. He just went hysterical and ran away. This is a horse who is extremely sensitive, frightened of hurting himself and hates all fence wire, and yet at that time, he would have gone through*

that wire without any hesitation just to make sure I couldn't get near him."

Frédéric realised he would get nothing out of Templado by using traditional methods. Everything had to be negotiated, even the simplest things. To get him to go from A to B, they always had to make detours instead of going the shortest way. *"We were still new to liberty training, believing that if we were simply kind to the horses, everything would be fine. But Templado's obvious distress under his rebellious exterior led us to think about new ways of working. We felt it was impossible to get through to his deep suffering by traditional teaching. Up to then, we had been too focused on a horse and rider relationship based on our own personal experience and on bits and pieces of systematised riding techniques. I don't mean this to reflect in any way on this sort of approach, which usually works well. A great number of top level riders have proved and are still proving that one can do good, efficient work based on both horse and rider knowing*

and remaining in their place. But with Templado, this wasn't enough. He was too rebellious. He saw his freedom as too important to be sacrificed in some codified, hierarchichal relationship."

At that time Frédéric mainly used liberty training with the geldings who normally have a less dominating and more flexible character.

"Let me do it and I will explain." If Templado had been able to express himself, that is surely the sentence he would have used.

Magali and Frédéric tried to put themselves in his place in order to work out what he was trying to tell them. *"If only for a couple of minutes at a time, we tried to see ourselves as he saw us. The barrier he put between us was like the one between humans and aliens, based mainly on lack of knowledge and misunderstanding of the other. Now, misunderstanding places the horse in an intolerable situation much more so than mistreatment. If he is mistreated, a horse always ends up by resigning himself to it. He lowers his head, withdraws into himself and takes punishment without reacting. On the other hand, an animal who doesn't understand what is being asked of him ends up in a state of fear. Templado's hypersensitivity caused him to be taken over by a panicky fear, an ill-defined anxiety that was almost autistic."* To break the ice which separated them, Magali and Frédéric first of all just wanted to prove that they meant him no harm. As simple as that

might seem, it was no easy matter. *"The mere contact of a hand about to stroke him would make him jump… and take refuge at the other end of his stall. You can imagine what liberty training sessions were like!"* However, they were not discouraged and they determined to find out what Templado liked, what he hated, what pleased him and what made him revolt. *"It was a question of reading what his nostrils, ears, eyes and general attitude had to tell us, whether he was happy or not, satisfied or not."*

By watching and listening, Frédéric and Magali came to understand the message Templado wanted to communicate. Since he needed complete liberty in order to feel at ease, they left him free to guide them wherever he wanted to take them. And the horse took them towards game-playing. Reluctant to work and impossible to control, Templado only accepted a relationship with humans in the context of a sort of play which freed him from any constraint, while offering him the choice of whether or not to apply the rules he had drawn up himself.

When given his liberty in the riding school, he played with Frédéric only when he decided to. Sometimes, without any explanation, he would turn on his heel and take refuge in the blind, fearful panic which filled him whenever he felt lost. *"His acceptance was conditioned by a calculated reserve. For example, when I called him to come to me, he would take a certain pleasure in taking one or two steps towards me. I even felt he was dying to*

■ Wild games at the foot of the Lubéron Alps.

come to me at a gallop. However, if he tried a third step, he suddenly realised he had gone too far and had allowed himself to become too familiar with me, and this put his sacrosanct freedom in jeopardy. So he drew back and went off as far as possible from me. And that was the end of the session."

Over time, Templado began to play more and with greater ease. A start had been made but progress was haphazard. Templado's panic reactions were remplaced by jerky movements and, little by little, panic gave way to confidence which, by gradual stages, began to take root. But each tiny bit of progress could be washed away in an instant, destroyed by his vague desire for freedom and what remained of his anger. Put together, they often overwhelmed him. One step forward, three steps back. Go back to start. Then suddenly a giant leap forward, only to go back to where they were before. Still, it was better than nothing, even though, on the merest whim, Templado could untie all the bonds you thought you had built up. In the space of five minutes, he was capable of destroying a month's work of hard-won progress on the pretext that Frédéric had tried to put on an unwelcome turn of speed. *"He forgave me nothing. The slightest error, the slightest faux pas on my part, and I was made to pay dear. He immediately put up the barriers and made me understand that I had burnt my bridges,"* says Frédéric.

■ You can't always be good at everything…

At this rate, progress was slow, almost to the point of desperation. Many people would have given up and pinned a sign on Templado's back saying "absolutely irretrievable". But because Frédéric and Magali put no real hope in this horse who was obsessed with freedom, and since he was not destined for anything in particular, they had no particular achievement in mind. They took what there was to take, if and when Templado saw fit to give them something. And, through the cycle of progress and failure, they took note, thought about it, discussed it, and tried again another way. In short, they tried to understand why, when and how Templado said yes; and why, when and how Templado said no.

"Templado made us think in a constructive way which never veered into an unhealthy fixation. I think that is what saved us. It has to be said that we didn't have the time. What with working

■ Let's take time out to think about it…

our performance horses and organising our tours, we had other things to do than get ourselves into a state over him. It is quite probable that, if we had worked with Templado with a definite objective in mind and within a specific time limit, the pressure and the need for a quick result would have made us take a different approach. We would have taken more risks, which would have made us make more mistakes. But in our case, we were happy just to follow the clues he gave us, to take the time to understand them and leave him enough time to accept us in his environment."

Humility, modesty and patience paid off. Little by little, Templado ended up by offering them a great deal of his confidence. From time to time, he would willingly place one knee on the ground. He would even attempt a few *cabrades*, rearing up hesitantly. Although he couldn't yet hold the position very well, he seemed to be enjoying this new game that Frédéric proposed to him.

Only a short time before, he had been the only master of the game but now he let Frédéric lay down different rules, on condition, of course, that he could keep his right to veto the whole thing!

Right-hand page
■ Templado posing in front of a gigantic portrait of himself, painted by Frédéric on the stable wall.

5

The Crinières d'Or 93, the revelation

At the end of 1992, Tavel was a hive of activity. Pierre Lapouge, the organiser of the famous equestrian show Crinières d'Or (Golden Manes) had asked Magali, Estelle and Frédéric to come up with a few numbers that he could put into his next show. This was a tremendous career opportunity for them and not to be missed on any account, because he might not ask again...

So, preparations began for the Crinières d'Or 93. Magali and Estelle worked on the choreography and quickly put together a three-handed number: Estelle dancing while Magali danced around her on Amoroso. In the meantime, Frédéric got his paintbox out and sketched some future numbers in order to persuade Pierre Lapouge to sign them up. He slipped a sketch of Templado into his portfolio of drawings, with his mane flowing free and a red shawl tied around his chest. This was deliberate on Frédéric's part because he knew that, for ages now, Pierre Lapouge had been on the lookout for a number that was truly unique and that would provide a few moments of pure magic for the spectators.

Frédéric thought it was worth trying, in the hope that Templado's portrait might strike Pierre Lapouge as the very horse he was looking for. It was a bit of a risk though – if Pierre Lapouge fell for the horse on paper, the real Templado would have to be made ready for the occasion, which was not going to be easy. Templado was certainly making progress but he was nowhere near ready to perform. He was only just beginning to go to Frédéric when he was called... and then only if he wanted to!

The reaction was instantaneous. Pierre Lapouge insisted on coming to Tavel to see if this horse really existed. He would also take the opportunity to look at the other numbers in rehearsal and see if they were up to scratch. For Magali, Estelle and Frédéric, there was too much at stake for the whole weight of success or failure to be placed on Templado's shoulders. Templado simply had to charm Pierre Lapouge, no matter how. And so the three of them worked on the sequence of the numbers they would show Pierre Lapouge so that nothing could possibly worry Templado when it came to his turn.

They needn't have worried so much. The moment the horse emerged from his stall, Pierre Lapouge fell in love with him – love at first sight. He wanted Templado in the show no matter how little he had been trained. Just a brief appearance, if necessary – just enough to light up the eyes of an audience who knew about horses. Templado was good enough to show Pierre Lapouge that he could do a few exercises tolerably well, like the *cabrade* (rearing up) and the *révérence* (taking a bow).

Pierre Lapouge returned to Tavel as happy as a sandboy for he had just found the horse of the year and, what's more, this jewel would be shown exclusively at the Crinières d'Or show.

■ One of the first appearances at the Crinières d'Or (Golden Manes).

The great day approached and with it came a horde of questions to be added to Frédéric's already considerable doubts. "What have I got myself into? What is Templado capable of? How far can I get him to go? How is he going to react in front of a lot of strangers in a place he's never seen before?"

There was no answer to any of these questions so Frédéric had no other choice but to wait for the fateful evening to find out if he was right or wrong in rushing into things. Discussing it with Magali, they agreed that, in the worst possible scenario, even if Templado went and did exactly what he felt like doing, Frédéric could always pretend he was stage-managing the whole thing. After all, he could be seen as getting his horse to express himself freely! And anyway, this would only make Templado look more beautiful and more impressive.

It was certainly true that he was breathtaking to look at, especially his mane which trailed down below his shoulders. This alone was enough to create an illusion, just in case…

22nd January 1993. Backstage, Templado was nervous. He wondered what on earth he was doing here. Frédéric knew his horse was tense but was reassured to know that they would be on first, opening the show. All they had to do was one lap at a gallop. *"Just a brief appearance – just enough to light up the eyes of an audience who know about horses,"* Pierre Lapouge had said.

The curtains opened and suddenly they both had to face the brutal reality of being in the ring in front of a crowd eager to see the first number of the new Crinières d'Or show.

"As soon as I let him go, in the middle of the stage, I realised that what I had here was a horse who was a true performer," Frédéric remembers.

Left-hand page, top
■ Templado and Frédéric with dancers from the Oro troupe, Avignon 1995.
Bottom
■ Dao and Zenete together, Avignon 2002.
Right-hand page, top
■ Templado at the Crinières d'Or of 2001.
Bottom left
■ End of a number: Zenete circling freely around Dao.
Bottom right
■ Zenete takes a bow.

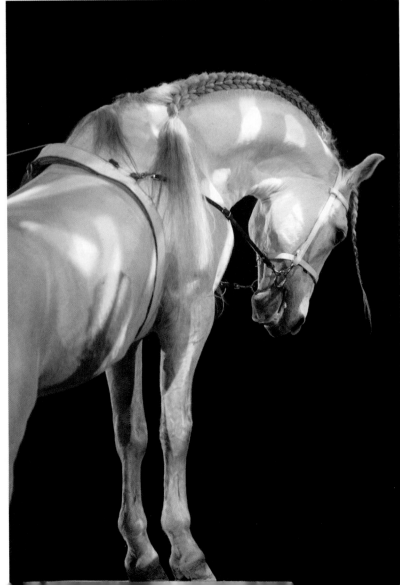

In front of three thousand spectators, Templado stretched up to his full height. Even if he didn't know exactly why he was there, he knew he was there to amaze. He crossed the stage, proud and erect, with a supple, flowing, high-stepping gait that he had been careful to keep to himself up to now. It was as if he wanted to kill two birds with one stone: to astound Frédéric and charm his audience – and it *was* his audience for, although he had never seen any of them before, he behaved as if they were old friends.

Frédéric was flabbergasted and stood there, in the middle of the ring, watching his horse enjoy this new game. Forgetting to keep up the pretence of directing the number, his astonishment slowly gave way to joy.

As for Templado, it had not immediately dawned on him that the situation was incongruous to say the least. Suddenly, he realised that he was all alone in this enormous ring, in the middle of nowhere, and in a confusion of light and sound which blinded and deafened him. Where was his friend who usually came to play with him at home? He searched around, couldn't see him and was seized by fright. Frédéric was his only real safe haven, even if he had never told him so. What was he going to do if Frédéric wasn't there any more? And then he saw him, at the other end of the ring. Like a lost child, Templado ran over to him, only too happy to have found his faithful companion at last.

Now Frédéric understood. In a few seconds, everything in Templado's world had turned upside-down. Faced by so many anonymous admirers, he felt at liberty. He could parade up and down and show off his fabulous mane without anyone saying anything about it, except to express their gratitude. But it was all just an act for, paradoxically, this crowd of strangers frightened him as much as it flattered his ego. His only ally in this uncertain world was Frédéric, the only one he already knew.

It only took one evening for the bond to be formed – a solid bond that could not be broken.

6

Who is the master?

The morning after the Crinières d'Or, everything had changed. The mist that up to now had enshrouded Templado began to clear. That morning Frédéric knew that Templado was a real performance horse. He also realised that the horse's behaviour the previous evening had given him a glimpse of how positive their relationship could turn out to be. His uncertain ideas about the horse's future faded away and were replaced by deep, well-founded convictions.

The thing was not to give in to the temptation to speed up the training, for the road to an *entente cordiale* is paved with obstacles that have to be carefully avoided.

There was only one way to get out of this maze of difficulties and this was for Frédéric to go on the same way as before and never assume the role of the accomplished trainer, or even as any sort of trainer. Templado had to be taken as he was, with all his energy and passion. Frédéric would use what he had already learned from Templado in order to bring them together and they would both have to go through a good deal of self-questioning in order to progress.

Frédéric says, *"Today, because of the experience I have gained with Templado and my other horses, I do things differently,*

faster, with less hesitation and soul-searching. But at the time,
didn't have the right key to decode everything the horse was telling
me. I had no other choice but to let myself be swept along by his
own wishes and pick up bits and pieces of explanation on the way.
That said, this pragmatic training was very beneficial. It enabled
us to get to know each other and learn mutual respect."

It was a sort of *ad hoc* training where there was room
for errors of interpretation and misunderstanding. One
evening, for example, in the wings, when both of them were
waiting to go on, Templado panicked because Frédéric began to
bend down. *"At home, it was a code between us, a code for start-*
ing a game. As soon as I crouched down, the horse would cut and
run. Since he was running free, he could do this… But, that
evening, I had to bend down to pick up my stick that I had
dropped. He thought it was his cue to bolt, even though he was
being held on a rein. He didn't hesitate for a second. He pulled so
hard that he snapped the rein and charged off at full gallop as he
would have done in the outdoor school," Frédéric remembers.
"Half in play, half in panic, his action reflected a flagrant misun-
derstanding between us on a specific point of our rules and for
which I was wholly to blame. He was just applying the rules that

had been laid down. It was up to me then to show him that the same signal can mean different things in different situations."

In the long term, these little hiccoughs turned out to be salutary. Templado didn't hold it against his assiduous pupil if occasionally he strayed from the straight and narrow. As for Frédéric, he took the time to analyse and unravel his mistakes and change his approach. He realised that he had to segment and break down every single movement of a new exercise so that the pyramid of learning that was being built could not be shaken. If not, like a house of cards, it would collapse and force him to start all over again.

Their individual roles were becoming clearly defined. Frédéric, the pupil, now had the right to propose new ideas. But he had no illusions about this. He knew perfectly well that Tempado would always have the last word, for he was the one who ultimately decided if he was ready or not for a specific exercise. *"I took all sorts of precautions when embarking on new exercises because it was like holding a bomb that kept having to be defused. For example, the mere fact of touching him on the foreleg to indicate the beginning of a* jambette *(raising one foreleg) or a* révérence *(going down on one knee) could spark off one of those outbursts of fear which I could do nothing to counteract. He would pull his foreleg away violently and bolt to the other end of the outdoor school, snorting. During the following weeks, it would be impossible to ask him to do the same figure again. For days on end we would return to the simplest exercises which he had already understood and mastered, and which he had no apprehension about, so that we could start off once again on a solid basis, free from any misunderstanding."*

Playing this sort of game demands patience, humility and perseverance. The proof of its effectiveness was that, after two years, Templado finally agreed to lie down. Frédéric had waited for this without ever showing the least sign of exasperation which could have jeopardised all the painstaking progress that had been made.

It was a year after the 93 Crinières d'Or when this revolution took place. One day, in the Tavel riding school, Templado lay down at Frédéric's feet, as relaxed as he could be.

"In order to realise the importance of this, one has to understand that a horse only lies down when he feels safe from danger, in a reassuring environment that is familiar to him. Since a horse's only means of defence is flight, when he is lying down he is completely defenceless, because he can no longer escape if threatened. For Templado – fractious and mistrustful, always suspicious of everything and anything – lying down was proof that he had complete trust in me. He gave himself up to me, accepting my presence as protection."

■ Make no mistake, you don't get a horse to lie down by pulling on its mane. Here, Frédéric prevents Templado getting his feet caught in his long mane which is always kept plaited, except for performance or for photographs.

This unexpected gift was without doubt the most intense moment of their whole story. Two long years of painstaking work summed up in one precious moment. However Frédéric very nearly gave up on more than one occasion.

"Two years is a long time, very long indeed… Some people will tell you that it's time wasted. It's true that there are a good many tried and tested methods which enable you to get a horse to lie down within a quarter of an hour. But, knowing Templado, I would never have taken the risk of using them on him. If I had, I would have set him against me forever for forcing him to do something against his will. That day, I had proof that everything comes to he who waits. Once horses have felt that they can lie down in safety, they can do it again and again without the least hesitation. You gain their confidence and therefore, in the long term, you save time. You work together in a spirit of good understanding rather than in constant conflict. And this is much more agreeable and enables you to go much further as well."

From the day Templado lay down, the final ditch that separated Frédéric from his horse had been crossed. The ties that bound them were tangibly strengthened. Because Templado had given him complete confidence, Frédéric gained confidence in himself. After so much trial and error, he finally knew he was on the right path. And he persevered with this way of working which he could now formulate clearly: *"Even if horses don't really understand what you want them to do at that particular moment, it's enough to suggest things very subtlely. If you make carefully formulated suggestions, one day they end up by responding positively. This way of working enables them to assume their own responsibilities. We listen to them and take their opinion into account. In the case of Templado, who prized his freedom above all, this was decisive."*

Knowing he was on the right track, Frédéric gained a certain amount of ease. His requests were more frank and much less hesitant. Templado understood them better and his reactions were more and more positive. Both parties became more confident in their respective roles. Together, they were finding their way into new territory. And because Frédéric seemed to master things, Templado ended up by relying on him. He had spent so many years paving the way for Frédéric, that it was quite natural now to pass the baton on to him. And today, his trust in Frédéric is so firmly rooted that nothing and no one, except Frédéric, can put that in doubt.

However, there was one thing that could have broken the whole peace process. If Frédéric had asked Templado to lie down a second time in the minutes that followed the action, or even the day after, it could have been a fatal error.

But he didn't. Out of respect for his horse and from his own experience, Frédéric avoided this pitfall. He knew that, even if Templado had understood the exercise, he would have to wait a few short weeks for him to lie down again, without putting any pressure on him to do so. That was of no consquence; they had the time. Remember the adage: *"everything comes to he who waits."*

With a few essential details added to this, everything was ready for Templado to get a taste for this new exercise. He needed a private place, with as little noise as possible, in which he felt at ease. The ground had to be soft, for if he were to hurt himself by slumping onto hard earth, that would be the end of lying down for quite a while. Therefore, the first trials took place in the covered riding school, away from intruders and extraneous noise.

Frédéric, using all his diplomacy, then got his horse to lie down in other places, on other types of ground and in other situations. Over the following months, Templado lay down in the sand of the outdoor school, in the grass of the garden and in front of other people. It took another year before Frédéric felt Templado was ready to lie down in performance.

1994: the chariot race

It had been several months now that work had been going really well between Templado and Frédéric. Their recent friendship was still a little shaky. It would have been easy to spoil everything by some stupid challenge. And yet…

One day, a contract fell into their lap that Chaps, the stunt man, could not fulfil because he was doing another show. It consisted of getting together a *poste* (standing on the backs of two horses) and a Roman chariot pair. Frédéric was excited by the idea since he loved acrobatic riding. He hadn't done either stunt for some time and he was missing it. The question was which horses to chose. Ever since he had gone towards liberty training and *haute école* dressage, he didn't have a single horse that was trained in this sort of acrobatic riding. Never mind, he would train them. After all, it was a simple matter to teach a horse to gallop in a straight line. How many dozen had he trained to do this in the past? However, when the horses were Templado or Amoroso, it was quite a different matter!

All the more so since, a few months back, a first experiment with a turnout and a professional driver had resulted in a qualified failure. Templado, chosen for his amazing looks, was brought in to complement a spike that had been put together for the Cheval Passion event in Avignon. He had to slip in between four other horses, two of whom were harnessed on either side of him and the other two harnessed behind. Templado felt constricted by the traces and sandwiched in and he lashed out furiously. However dangerous it looked, the experiment was nevertheless not as disastrous as all that. The driver knew his job inside out and was clever enough to keep Templado in his place while not hurting his mouth, which would have antagonised him even more.

After this somewhat doubtful experience, Frédéric decided to prepare Templado for harnessing, being careful not to make any mistakes which could cost him dear in terms of mutual respect. He started by classic long rein work but the horse, who was used to always having Frédéric in his field of vision when they played together, was surprised to feel him behind him, invisible but very near his croup. He was disorientated and, after a few steps, suddenly turned to face Frédéric who, so as not to make the situation worse, stayed as cool as ice. Templado could easily get his feet caught in the rein by turning around like that and it was absolutely necessary to avoid getting the reins tangled up.

But, after a few sessions, Templado proved to his master that their trusting relationship was now unshakeable. He finally accepted this new game with good humour and energy. And when Frédéric harnessed him to the Roman chariot, Templado threw himself into the game with such enthusiasm that it looked like it could be a new vocation, even more so since Amoroso had no taste for being put in the traces.

The result was that Templado was bowled over by the chariot race, without bowling over the chariot when they were going at full gallop!

Above ■ The spike, led by Mr Dourouze, is made up only of members of the "Perdigon family": two fillies at the pole and three stallions at the splinter bar, with Templado in the centre.

7

Freedom above all

When he was nine, Templado finally reached the age of reason. He was two years behind the rest of his year even though he had begun his training with the Delgado-Pignon school at just the right moment five years ago.

Throughout that period he had shown himself to be the typical bad pupil: stubborn, rebellious and undisciplined. But, behind the facade of violent revolt, was exceptional intelligence and sensitivity.

It was true to say that he had given everyone a very hard time, but this was all in the past. All the rebelliousness of youth had been pardoned because of the enormous potential that he was thought to have. Under that shell of awkward, uneasy adolescence, there was a huge capacity for trust, respect, obedience and friendship.

■ Work session: Templado being put through his exercises. On the left, a piaffer; in the centre, a *levade*; on the right, a *révérence*. Not always fun, but necessary…

Over the previous five years, Templado had done his utmost to provide Frédéric and Magali with a real treasure trove. By means of their observation of and dialogue with this very atypical horse, their technical progress, their approach to stallions and their whole understanding of horses had taken a huge leap forward.

Frédéric and Templado were finally mature enough for a relationship that was healthy, frank and truly friendly; a relationship that had been developed over those five years by dint of really hard work. Templado was now free from all his anxieties and fits of rebellion. He would play with Frédéric without a second thought, on condition that Frédéric left him a share of the responsibility in defining the rules. For if there is one issue on which he has never wanted to concede the tiniest point, it is his freedom. *"He is the opposite of his brother, Fasto, a good hardworking pupil who wants only to do his level best to come up to my expectations and for me to take full charge. Templado only grants my requests insofar as they correspond to a game whose framework we have drawn up together. Then and only then will he show how much he really loves to play."*

Frédéric is walking the tightrope of liberty training to try and find the perfect balance between too much liberty and not enough. And he has found an infallible compromise.

"Game-playing in liberty training is like a holiday and when you're on holiday all the time, you don't know how to enjoy it any more." Basing himself on this piece of common sense, Frédéric alternates play sessions and work sessions on the long

rein as often as possible, thereby putting the brakes on Templado's desire for freedom which could easily turn into insolent behaviour. *"Nowadays we work in such close partnership that I allow him to take too many liberties with me. For example, at the beginning of a play session, he does a lap round the ring at the gallop to show me that he's independent. When we're alone together, this doesn't matter. Quite the contrary, we're having fun. But as soon as I put him with other horses, he takes advantage of his privileged position to stir things up in the group. He will bite or get a horse to be undisciplined. In short, I have to take him in hand from time to time. And this makes him appreciate the game sessions that follow even more. We are like two people making up after a quarrel, happy to play together again and enjoy each other to the full."*

So Templado regularly has to endure a long rein session. Of course, he doesn't like being humiliated like this. He, the great Templado, has to grin and bear this moral lesson and work seriously. As soon as he sees Frédéric coming to his stall, armed with all his 'torture instruments', his eyes glint with anger. And when Frédéric puts on the roller, the bands and the bit, he lowers his ears as a sign of vexation. For the first few turns around the ring, he pouts in exasperation. He would just love to get rid of Frédéric who is right behind him. He turns round to face him and to try and tangle up those cursed reins. Then, believing that he has put his master in awe of him, he rears up and comes down to the side. *"Just like when he was young,"* says Frédéric philosophically as he calmly gets the horse back under control in the long reins.

■ A reward is guaranteed, now we can play.

"That's his bad loser side. He complains for the sake of complaining and to see which of us is really controlling the game. He will try anything to get out of the constraints of work. But then, when he sees that I know him too well and that there is no room for negotiation, he ends up by giving in. The irony is that, once he's started work, he becomes very conscientious and forgets all of his bad will! But he always starts off by making sure I know that he is quite capable of sending me packing!"

When he concentrates on the exercises Frédéric asks him to do, Templado pouts – he really hates wearing a collar! However, he knows that if he bends to Frédéric's wishes, the reward promised to hard-working pupils will be given – work sessions always end with well-deserved recreation. As soon as Frédéric takes off the reins and bit, the equilibrium between them is instantly restored. Templado stops pouting and his teasing eyes sparkle with joy. He now does anything he can to take the initiative – all in fun, all in play.

Templado has the spirit of a revolutionary; he is a tease and he loves being a troublemaker. He relishes those moments of confusion for which he alone is responsible and which enable him, paradoxically, to assert himself as Frédéric's best pupil and favourite. For as soon as he makes trouble among his playmates, he comes back to Frédéric to prove his attachment for him, his goodwill, and above all to emphasise the impertinence of the others who are the ones creating havoc!

There is only a fine line between these little masquerades and a real clash of wills between horses disputing leadeship, all the more so since all the horses Frédéric does liberty training with are stallions. If anyone shows too possessive or exclusive an attitude towards their master, becomes a bit aggressive or shows a dash of domination, then the warpaint goes on. Such conflict could do incalculable damage if Frédéric did not act as the negotiator.

The best example of a struggle for leadership between two stallions is the one that for years opposed Templado and his elder half-brother, Amoroso.

Templado is a horse with a dominant character who knows the rules of the hierarchy well. Amoroso on the other hand is an aggressive horse who was rejected by his own kind. Sold at the age of 6 months, Amoroso grew up away from the company of other horses. When he later came back to his birthplace, he had not therefore been taught the necessary 'horse education' and this remained a terrible gap in his schooling.

Amoroso was extremely unsociable and showed violent aggression towards his fellows while, on the other hand, he was extremely possessive about Frédéric and Magali and it would have been dangerous to put this in question.

■ Don't I look like a handsome Andalusian?

However, one day, because they were going to have to perform side by side, Frédéric put Templado and Amoroso together. By way of damage limitation, he took them out in reins. This experiment proved to be extremely dangerous, for each stallion tried to impose his authority on the other. Templado because he knew he was the leader, and Amoroso because, as a militant anarchist, he refused to accept any sort of hierarchy. Templado tried to frighten his brother, pushing him and rearing up in front of him then rejoining Frédéric. Not put off by this, Amoroso was already at Frédéric's side, to give back as good as he got. He tried to bite and kick Templado who did the same, trying to show his authority – not out of any real malice, but because of who he was. After a few attempts at a *coup d'état*, the aggressive anarchist ended up by surrendering to Templado who was decidedly much stronger.

Since then, Frédéric regularly lets out Amoroso, Templado and Fasto together, without reins. Amoroso is still just as vindictive, so the situation is still very strained. Frédéric is extremely vigilant, keeping the two old enemies in their place and above all making them stay there. As for gentle young Fasto, all this is quite beyond him and nothing is going to make him get mixed up with these big brother ogres.

Templado is the uncontested leader of all the stallions. Even Amoroso the anarchist bends his head to him. Templado wanted to be leader, won the leadership and plays his role to the full. Nothing and no one can take his crown away from him.

Estelle's lovely brown bay, Guisot, was the odd one out in the stables. For some mysterious genetic reason, he was one of the few sons of Perdigon to have a coat so dark it looked almost like ebony. Knowing he was different, Guisot would take advantage of this to show off unashamedly. He played with his expressive head, his massive neck and his attractive rounded body, to attract the eye of the passer-by. Not only did he love to show off but he passed from the hands of Estelle to those of Frédéric with no worry. With Estelle he worked on dressage and from Frédéric he learned the rules of liberty training so as to be able to join his big brothers in a multi-coloured performance number. It has to be said that, despite the fact that Guisot was almost black and Fasto was white, there was a striking resemblance between them and the age difference would not be noticeable in a few months time. With a year between them, Fasto (9 years old) was already a professional. He had been performing for a season with his elder brother Templado and sometimes even with Zenete or Amoroso.

Guisot, as studious and attentive as Fasto was at the same age, showed a real will to progress further every day. When

he was alone with Frédéric, he loved to listen, to come to him, to rear up, and was even starting to want to lie down. It was time for him to have his stage *début*, in the company of a brother. Since Fasto was still not mature enough, it fell upon Templado to initiate Guisot into liberty work as a pair. Templado was an expert on the subject and would know exactly how to show Guisot where his place was. And if the young novice was unwilling to take his place, Templado would put him there, firmly if necessary.

Having relaxed Guisot, Frédéric went to fetch Templado. While they introduced themselves, he preferred to keep the old rascal on a halter as the naive uncultured youngster came up to sniff him and say hello. Templado was exasperated by such rudeness and lack of respect. His neck swelled up to twice its size, he snorted and blew as loudly as he could and stretched up to his full height. The gentle little upstart who had come to greet him fell back and shrank visibly in size! In a fraction of a second, Guisot had understood where authority lay and submitted totally to his leader, without any negotiation.

■ Bowing to the audience, in the Massey garden in Tarbes; from left to right, Templado, Amoroso, and Aétès.

70

■ Guisot, rather intimidated by the imposing figure of his big brother.

The next day, Frédéric went a little further in bringing them into contact. He let the two horses loose together. Proud he may have been but Guisot was no fool. He had learnt his lesson. He kept his distance and, out of the corner of his eye, took note of what his brother was saying to him and tried to obey him to the letter. In one short session, Guisot fell into step without any voices being raised or any conflict. By his mere presence and self-assurance, Templado established his superiority from the word go. He took the upper hand psychologically, without aggression, in such a way that Guisot did not even try to enter into conflict with him.

A commotion in the stables

It has to be admitted that, in the stalls, Templado is a really difficult customer. He is temperamental, capricious, authoritarian, taciturn and independent to the point of being a loner. His Majesty does not like to be disturbed when he is at home.

His rages are famous throughout the stables. All the horses have been on the wrong end of one of them at least once in their lives. But, once the anger has passed, Templado sees the funny side of it.

These few memorable and not unfunny examples give us a glimpse into his really unusual character.

One day, after riding the giant Famoso, Magali returned him to his stall. She was rather concerned by a small scab on a tendon and told Frédéric about it. Hurrying out of the stall, she left the door wide open, thinking that Frédéric would be over in a moment to take a look at Famoso. Frédéric, on the other hand,

was busy doing something else (absent-mindedly perhaps), forgot about Famoso and went off into the barn next door. Magali, meanwhile, was already back on horseback and, from the outdoor school where she was working, heard a frightful din coming from Famoso's stables. Knowing Frédéric, she suspected that he had forgotten to close the stable door. She dismounted and hurried to the stable. And what did she find there? Famoso's stall was still wide open as she had expected. But the horse hadn't moved. From his great height – 1.75 m at the withers – he was calmly fiddling with the hay placed in the corner of his litter. All the din was coming from Templado. The stable leader was mad with rage that a door should be open. Upset at not being able to get out to go and explain to Famoso that he, Templado, was the master, Templado was kicking, whinnying, snorting and groaning – getting hysterical in fact. He threw himself against the wall, trying to push it, then to break it by kicking it with his hind legs. All to no effect. The door would not give. Luckily, he thought, that great big simpleton, Famoso, hasn't thought about going walkabout. For if he had, wall or no wall, he would take great pleasure in jumping on him. The great big simpleton in question may indeed have placed one tentative horseshoe outside the stall, but faced by the explosive fury of his sovereign who was turning into a tyrant, he doubtless thought it more prudent to turn round and eat his hay, as if nothing had happened!

"These fits of authority happened from time to time," *Frédéric says, still amazed by their occurrence. "As if he couldn't stand being put in front of a* fait accompli. *Even yesterday, we put Amoroso next to Templado instead of his usual neighbour. This made Templado just about as furious as when Famoso's stall was left open. He would have smashed the whole place to smithereens!"*

Brigitte is someone who has been employed by Magali and Frédéric for a long time and knows her job backwards. She has taken care of twenty or so stallions for several years and she knows all their little ways. However, one day, she called for help. Frédéric heard her and rushed to Templado's stall where the cry was coming from. First of all, he saw the horse, right up against his manger and not looking friendly at all. Then, trapped under the manger in a corner of the stall, he saw poor Brigitte who looked too scared to move. It was for a good reason – Templado was menacing her and simply refusing to let her leave. He was ready to use his teeth if necessary and even give her a good kick up the backside.

What had happened? Templado's stall is his castle and he cannot stand anyone coming in or disturbing him without a valid reason. Anyone who does comes in to disturb his sacrosanct privacy had better justify his presence with a good deal of authority from the word go, or else he won't make things easy for him. If he senses any weakness on the part of the intruder, he will have no mercy and throw him out. Worse still, if he realises that he is dealing with someone who is afraid of him, he is even more annoyed and will take a sadistic pleasure in trapping him in a corner and not leaving him any way of getting out.

Now, Brigitte goes into Templado's stall at least five times a day. He knows her, recognises her and likes her. He knows that when she comes it is always for a good reason: she brings his hay, feeds him and grooms him carefully. She is always nice to him, takes good care of him and treats him with the honour that is due to him.

But that day, she must have arrived at an unusual time for her and he must have been surprised to see her. She must also have been surprised at his unusual reaction and, without putting up any resistance, let herself be imprisoned by the horse without knowing what had got his back up.

To help the poor girl get out of her hiding-place, Frédéric called Templado to order. He raised his voice and gave him a good telling off. Whatever Templado's reasons might be, this sort of behaviour would not be tolerated. He should learn some manners. But Frédéric could not stop himself smiling when he left. Templado loved to play the big boss! *"Like the day when he gave little Laury a terrible fright,"* he remembers with a grin. *"The boy knew the horse well and was used to going into his stall. But that day, Templado must have wanted either to play or to frighten him. The boy was so scared that he simply jumped over the wall of the stall. And I found him running down the stable aisle like a madman, with his heart going 100 miles an hour!"* Yes indeed, Templado loves to play the big boss, but it's all bluff because, when it comes down to it, he is much too gentle to go too far.

Right-hand page
■ By the wall of a church in Velleron, in the Vaucluse region. Templado poses in front of a wrought iron sculpture dedicated to Saint Éloi, the patron saint of blacksmiths. The sculpture is made out of all sorts of horseshoes, even the most unlikely…

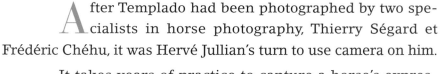

The soul
of a supermodel

After Templado had been photographed by two specialists in horse photography, Thierry Ségard et Frédéric Chéhu, it was Hervé Jullian's turn to use camera on him.

It takes years of practice to capture a horse's expression, whether he be still or in movement, and Hervé's predecessors knew all the ins and outs of the question. They took at least 1,000 photos each of Templado and it must have been wonderful to have the greatest supermodel of the equestrian world in front of the camera.

Templado had appeared in a wide range of advertisements. The glories of his mane even attracted the attention of shampoo manufacturers who were interested in the idea of comparing his tresses with human hair and had him perform for the cameras of their ad men.

Now it was the turn of the fashion world, who wanted to have photos of this horse on record for use on a future front cover. So Hervé Jullian, the fashion photographer, made his way down to Provence. His own artistic vision, together with the fact that he had chosen to work in black and white, was to produce some extremely original photos.

For the first session, it was decided not to stray too far from the posed work done in fashion studios. It was the chance to prove that a horse could be as professional as the very best supermodel.

The studio was to be a natural location, and we chose the old stone streets of Velleron. It is a charming village with over a dozen fountains scattered along the narrow lanes and in the shady squares. The ever-present sound of water is reminiscent of the peaceful courtyards of Spanish houses and made the setting even more perfect for our equine model with his Iberian roots.

We parked just below the village and walked up through the streets, escorted by Templado held by Frédéric on a simple halter rein. He walked nonchalantly, being used to changes of scene and unusual new environments. He was calm

and confident, with complete trust in his master. Suddenly, he scented something in the air. His nostrils dilated, his head lifted and his ears perked up. He whinnied and showed, only too visibly, how much that scent had excited him. In a proud trot he advanced, searching for the source of his excitement. A mare must have passed by there.

We had to cross the village like this with Templado immodestly showing off his virility. And then his nostrils no longer sensed the smell and he went off the boil, falling back into a gentle indolence.

We arrived at the the town hall square which everyone agreed was the perfect place – in the background was the Cambis castle with its impressive wrought iron gates.

Hervé got his cameras ready while Frédéric put the model in place. The mane like this, feet like that, shoulders straight, head like this. Hold it. Click. And it was all over. When Frédéric had put him in the position they wanted, the horse had stood there completely motionless and didn't move a muscle, just like a statue.

We moved from the wrought iron gates to the fountain in the middle of the square. There, Templado finally found something to arouse his curiosity. His stared at the fountain, intrigued by the water pouring into the stone bowl. He wasn't frightened, or at least if he was, he hid it very well. Any other horse would have sniffed the disquieting object and then turned to flee the danger. But Templado took it in his stride. After all, he could not lower himself to admit fear of something of so little importance. But neither could he take his eyes of the fountain so close to him. Frédéric spoke to him, asking him to take the pose. Torn between his new attraction for the fountain which seemed to be alive and his faithful adoration of his master, Templado went for a compromise. He would consent to raise his head to face the camera if he could stay there, next to the fountain. But it never came to that for the site was too dark and we decided to change to another fountain. The same procedure was repeated: Hervé got ready while Frédéric put the model in place. They wanted to take him three quarters on, from the back, head turned facing his croup, looking towards Hervé. No sooner said than done: the mane like this, the feet like that, shoulders to the right, head towards the camera. Templado let himself be placed. Click. The photos were done. It seemed so easy but it represented months of work. You should try it yourself someday. Put yourself behind your horse's croup and have him turn his head towards you without moving his haunches. Try to keep him in this fixed position while you walk back six metres… The best laid plans of mice and men…

Word had spread throughout the village and the inhabitants came out to see this horse, as free as air, but as still as marble and as handsome as a hero of Greek mythology. Unaware of the difficulty of the pose because it looked so natural, and not realising how much concentration it took from the horse as well as from his master, they approached the pair to offer their congratulations. Frédéric politely responded without taking his eyes off the horse for a second. If there was no eye contact, Templado would move and Frédéric would have to reposition him in the same place and in the same attitude. But he needn't have worried. At that moment, Templado didn't take any notice of the passers-by who were disturbing things. He was absorbed in his pose, only interested in Hervé Jullian's camera lens. Hervé was satisfied. He had got exactly what he needed. Templado was perfect.

On the way back, the same female scent attracted the stallion. He began to call her with a loud whinny. Hervé quickly got a camera out of his bag. Too late, Templado was already quiet again. And then, just when Hervé was putting his equipment away, he whinnied again as if he didn't want anyone to stare at him while he was giving vent to his feelings.

In order to make the shot more spontaneous, Frédéric took off the halter rein and distanced himself from Templado, in the hope that in a while he would whinny again. But he hadn't counted on the horse's professionalism. With the halter off, Templado forgot all about his stallion's instincts. He was a top model first and foremost. He concentrated on the job and looked at Frédéric as if to ask him to describe the scene he was to play. The mare,

whether she were in the vicinity or not, would have to wait until the end of the pose.

Seeing Templado in his new pose, Hervé abandoned the whole idea because the horse no longer seemed to want to whinny. Frédéric put the halter on again. Surprised that the session was already over, but not particularly upset, Templado let himself be led on the rein. But since work was over, now for the mare… and he started whinnying again!

A strange situation indeed, in which the horse, thinking he was acting for the best, did everything the wrong way round. But we couldn't hold it against him, because we were the ones who caused him to make the mistake.

The upshot of this was that there were no photos to record the scene.

A mudbath

Hervé Jullian had long wanted to take photos of Templado covered in mud. You might call this an artist's fancy but, in the fashion world, one must not forget that they have no compunction about putting models in mud in order to show off the beneficial effects of mudbaths!

So Templado went off to endure a most unusual photo session, all in the interests of fashion. But the question was: where to find the mud that would mess up his immaculate white coat.

The weather came to our aid. It was the beginning of May and, unusually for Provence, it had been raining so heavily that there were pools of water in the sand and grass. But there was a chill in the air and there was no question of letting Templado catch cold.

The solution was found in the outdoor school, which was swimming in water. The sand was regurgitating the liquid it could no longer absorb. It was the perfect place. So there was no need to go in search of a muddy pool. It was there, in front of the stables, only a few metres from the hot shower.

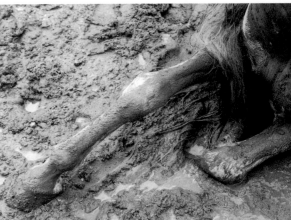

The hardest part was yet to come. How could Templado be persuaded to take part in this bizarre affair? How could he be induced to get down in that cold, filthy mud? Frédéric went to get his friend from the stall, apologising in advance for what he was about to inflict on him. He also explained that true professionals had to comply with all the trends in fashion or in the cinema, no matter how wild or fantastic they might seem.

Templado came out of his stall, white from head to toe. His mane and tail, freshly brushed, untangled and combed, floated around him. All of this whiteness would be sullied – and this was bad enough – but it would be a monster task to get him back to his original colour again, a challenge that would defy even the very best of shampoos. *"Oh well, never mind. One thing at a time,"* thought Frédéric. He took Templado to the outside school and, greeted by a sea of curious faces, Templado naturally assumed his star personality.

It was then that he looked at his companion in absolute astonishment. What on earth was he being asked to do? Was Frédéric serious? Could it be true? Was he going to have to lie down in that ghastly slush? For a moment, the star was lost. He wondered if his master – who was normally so sensible – had lost his reason. Never before had he played such a trick on him. What's more, when he was looking his best with all his hair loose, as he was now, he was absolutely forbidden to roll on the ground.

Consternation followed doubt. It was indeed true. Frédéric had gone completely off his head. Templado was bewildered but, to indulge the crazy whims of his friend, with good grace he did exactly what was asked of him. He delicately lowered one knee, then the other knee, and let himself down gently.

As if to confirm the fact that he had gone mad, Frédéric then spread the waterlogged sand all over Templado's back. But, even though he let his faithful horse think he was mad, Frédéric was nothing of the sort. He started with the flanks, then the croup and the withers before attacking neck and head.

Templado was completely bewildered. In his startled eyes one could read pity for Frédéric – that he should stoop to this! But, squatting in the mud, the boss seemed to be having a great time, plunging his hands into the sand and slapping the sticky brown mess all over Templado, even on his mane and tail, without missing a single strand of hair.

Hervé Jullian was lost in admiration at the stoicism of this animal who, whether out of intelligence or affection, was allowing his best friend to go completely crazy.

Suddenly, everything changed. One click of the camera and Templado understood. He noticed the photographer and realised he had been put in the mud for a good reason. How could he have doubted Frédéric for a single moment?

His eyes suddenly sparkled and his consternation gave way to amusement. In his absolute stillness, his whole body seemed to give off energy. He seemed to agree that brown suited him quite well. It showed off the shape of his body and the contours of his muscles. Quite happy with his new colour, Templado straightened and, without getting up, stretched out a back leg. Such intense vitality emanated from him that one could envisage how the movement would continue: it looked as if he was emerging from a fountain, ready to bound up in an instant.

Everyone was over the moon. Templado was enjoying himself too in his pose – half bronze statue, half real horse. Then, with a gesture and a word, Frédéric told him he could get up. He didn't have to ask twice – after all the ground was rather cold!

Once on his feet, the majestic horse moved his head about in an attempt to make his mane swirl about. But in vain. Hard as he tried, he was stupefied and enraged to find his mane weighed down by the mud that was plastered to his skin. It would not move and his heavy neck, flattened and not rounded as usual, could not find a way to get his mane to react. Templado went off into a trot as if to forget about this affront. But the weight on his tail put a brake on his *élan*. Now he was really annoyed and he tried walking round a bit pretending that nothing was wrong.

■ Aaah, a nice shower!

Frédéric knew that, in the space of a few seconds, the horse could go from carefree euphoria to the blackest of rages, so he hastily stepped in to remotivate him for the photo session. He called him several times to come to him. Still angry, Templado pretended not to hear but then temptation got the better of him. His friendship for Frédéric was worth much more than a fit of vanity. He turned and galloped up to him in his new brown coat.

For a while, he threw himself into the game and gave unstintingly of himself. He played with his master, with the camera, and for the audience. Then he played for himself, switching his brown mane back and forth and going into a gallop, enjoying the effect of polished stone that his mane now presented.

The bystanders applauded, loving the spectacle of this unbelievable horse who could change a situation to his own advantage and always show himself at his best.

Frédéric stroked him to say thank you and Templado realised that the session was over. He waited patiently for his master to run to the shower room, then followed him at a trot and immediately got under the hot shower to rid himself of the brown coat he had been given to wear.

The shampoo covered him in lather and Magali arrived to help. Two people were hardly enough to rub his mane clean and scrub his whole body and tail. Templado stood there and let them go ahead. After all, a massage like that was extremely pleasant. Without intending any offence to cosmetics manufacturers, clean hot water is so much better than a mudbath!

In front of the cameras

Frédéric had been contacted by Tissot, the Swiss watchmaker, who wanted Templado for a commercial and he had to prepare Templado for something very different from what he was used to. For the purposes of the ad, the horse had to respond to his master from at least 6 metres away, so that the latter would be off camera. It would take time for the horse to get used to the new rules that Frédéric was going to lay down.

For a final rehearsal, he took Templado into an enormous field nearby. When the moment came to let the horse loose in total liberty, he took all the usual necessary precautions to lessen the risks. With the help of Magali and Brigitte, he drew out a huge square around the horse. Three sides were formed by pieces of white rope and the fourth was represented by a wide ditch that bordered the field.

In the distance, a mare was grazing quietly. This didn't worry Frédéric because Templado was very serious when he was at work.

But that day, Templado the old pro had decided otherwise. He had scented the mare and with a wicked look in his eye, waited for Frédéric to distance himself. When he did so, Templado seized the opportunity and took off at full gallop. To everyone's astonishment, he jumped the ditch and headed in the direction of the siren who was calling him. At the speed he was going, no barrier was going to stop his determination to get where he wanted to go. His long mane was flying in all directions and they were worried that, in his frenzy, he might even tread on it and tear out hunks of the hair.

Fortunately, Frédéric had brought Flequillo along in case of necessity. This proved to be an excellent choice for he was one of the horses in the cossack stunt riding number and was an expert at top speed gallops. In a fraction of a second, Frédéric passed the halter rein around his neck like a pair of reins, jumped on his back and they went off like a bolt of lightning. It only took a short time to reach Templado and the mare who, for the moment, were eyeing each other from a distance.

It was not going to be easy... Templado was playing the part of Zorro and was ready to defend his new sweetheart against all-comers. He dared anyone to approach. He whinnied loudly, snorted like a mad thing, beat his forelegs on the ground and lifted up his tail with panache. In short, he pulled out all the stops... to such an extent that he forgot about his male instincts. Not for one moment did he try to approach the mare. He just wanted to defend her from unsuitable people, just like Zorro, protector of widows and innocent young girls.

This peculiar situation could have turned nasty and quick reactions were needed. Frédéric dismounted, preferring to keep Flequillo out of it, and Magali and Brigitte came to join him. All three now tried to keep Templado away from his pretty little ward. After a while, they persuaded him to see reason. Neither mare nor stallion was greatly upset by this and, almost without batting an eyelid, the mare went back to grazing and Templado returned to his master!

Once this high-spirited interlude was over, the rehearsal could take place calmly. They had to work fast because the day of the filming was fast approaching!

In the storyline of the Tissot ad, Templado had to walk slowly towards a child who was lying in the sand on a deserted beach. Once at his side, the horse had to slowly bend his head and sniff the child's neck. Then the child would get up, jump on the horse and both would gallop off towards the sea...

■ All right, I'll give my lungeing rein to Mathieu, but where has Fréd gone?

Filming the scene was a lot less romantic. Magali and Frédéric stood 12 metres away from each other, on either side of the horse, to 'send' and 'receive' the horse in turn. Templado had understood the rules of this new game. He knew that, even if Frédéric was far away and out of sight, he had to obey him as long as he could hear his voice. Magali held Templado until 'Action' was called. Templado searched for his master with his eyes and ears, trying to locate him. Suddenly, he could just make him out, quite a way away, camouflaged by some bushes.

Frédéric was worried because Templado was so used to coming to him at a gallop that it would be very difficult to slow him down to a more leisurely pace. And what if the horse kept his eyes on him all the time and forgot about the child lying on the ground? The Mistral – the strong Mediterrean wind – was whistling and this didn't help matters. Fortunately, the sound-track would be added later in the studios. Frédéric had to shout

88

■ On the beaches of Saintes-Maries, the film crew gets ready for the scene where Mathieu is taken into the water.

over the noise of the wind and make huge 'slow down' gestures to stop Templado from galloping. When the horse was within 6 metres of him, Frédéric gave him a sharp 'stop' sign and he stopped dead. The child was there, at his feet, with a sugar lump hidden in his hair. This trick worked the very first time, for Templado had understood what was expected of him. He bent down to get the sugar.

"Cut! One more time, please!" A few more takes and it was 'in the can'. But things were not so easy when it came to the final scene when the child had to jump up onto the horse and they would both dash off along the endless beach. Templado cannot stand having someone on his back, and it was an enormous risk even to put a flyweight on his back, just like that, with no safety precautions, and then ask him to gallop off... Templado's past record was a sure guarantee that this might end up

in hopeless chaos and with the child falling off. What's more, the child in question was Mathieu, Frédéric's younger brother. Frédéric was torn between the desire to initiate his brother into the world of stunt riding and the wish not to expose him to any unnecessary danger. So, by way of damage limitation, the scene was divided up into two distinct sequences: the mounting and the gallop. Templado would only figure in the first sequence and, to make it even safer, Frédéric advised Mathieu just to to grab Templado's mane and jump to the side of the horse, only pretending to mount. Then Amoroso would take Templado's place in the final scene. He was the perfect stand-in, being the very image of his brother, so no one would notice the switch. Magali had whitened Amoroso's mane to make it like Templado's but, in all other respects, the two horses were as like as two peas in a pod. The gallop would only be seen from a distance anyway, and studio editing would make the illusion complete.

During the shot, Templado, taking advantage of a moment of respite, went off by himself and then set off on a wild gallop towards his brother and the child. He obviously thought this was getting too serious and needed spicing up a bit!

■ Between two shots on the set of "Soirées sauvages", Jean-Luc Reichman is amused to see Templado showing that he's bored.

The professional

"Ah, the merry merry month of May…" Such was my first thought when I awoke at 6 a.m. on 10th May 2002. I am an early riser as soon as the weather starts getting warmer but that day I had trouble getting out of bed. The heating was on in my bedroom for it was like midwinter and it was pouring with rain outside. I was really worried that the photo session with Hervé Julian might have to be cancelled if the sky didn't clear.

At seven o'clock, over a cup of coffee, we were going through our schedule. The rain looked like stopping but the weather had been terrible recently and this did not augur well for the shoot we had planned. We had to take a quick decision. There was an icy chill in the air so we decided to forget Saintes-Maries-de-la-Mer and its deserted beaches and fall back on a less famous but very picturesque location: the Julien bridge.

This vestige of a long-gone era is still intact. It is an old Roman bridge leading to Bonnieux, just a few miles from Apt. Between its high arches runs the river Calavon. Pride of the region, the bridge and its river are visited by tourists who arrive there in their coachloads. They stay just long enough to take a few snaps with their disposable cameras and then pile back into their vehicles to continue on their way to the Roman castle. They don't even take the trouble to go down to the river and admire the beautiful workmanship of the little Roman bridge from underneath. Well, that's their loss – and our gain, for it meant we wouldn't be disturbed during our photo shoot.

We had reconnoitred the bridge the previous evening and evaluated the risk of letting Templado loose in this unusual location. From the top of the bridge, the little Calavon had looked insignificant. But once we were down below, this usually peaceful river showed itself to be flowing as fast as a torrent. Only a short time before, it had taken on board all the rain that had fallen and the water was rushing fast around the piles. That morning, it had been swollen by the stormy rains and had an earthy colour that made it impossible to see down to the mysterious depths of the little Calavon.

On either bank, the lush greenery and beaches of stones and pebbles polished by time and water bore witness to the spring tides. In some places, sand had turned the earth to a dark ochre. From above, looking down over the ancient Julien bridge, the view is lovely, but from down below it is lovelier still. However, a walk along the banks of the river is no easy matter. They are uneven, muddy in places, smooth and slippery in others, sometimes marshy in the midst of dense high bamboos… It is a place to be negotiated only by the keenest of those who are in search of picturesque landscapes.

It was a huge challenge. Even an experienced hiker would have trouble there. It was almost unthinkable to bring a horse there for a photo shoot, and to get him to go into the water would be sheer madness. He could easily take fright, slip on a smooth stone, fall against the base of a pile and hurt himself badly. As for letting him loose in this hostile environment, no one would risk it. Unless of course the horse was called Templado and his master was Frédéric Pignon.

For Templado is a real actor and was by far the best choice for this difficult part. No audition and no stand-in were called for. Templado is agile and attentive enough to adapt to the

requirements of any script. He could play the part of any stunt man under his director's orders, for his words were gospel.

Frédéric, using all the tact and diplomacy you need when talking to stars, showed him the set. The horse took his time before agreeing to go ahead. He looked around, sniffed the air and, in passing, attempted to steal some grass, which was much more interesting than those nasty-looking rocks he was going to have to negotiate next. So be it… The set met with his approval. He agreed to the terms and went surefootedly to the water's edge as if he already knew that he was going for a bathe.

His hooves were just touching the water when suddenly he changed his mind. He didn't want to do it any more, he wanted to renegotiate the terms. He stood there on the water's edge, firmly resolved not to budge unless concessions were made. The impresario spoke to him, stroking and caressing him at first and then telling him, in no uncertain terms, to pull himself together: *"What are you playing at? What sort of actor backs out like this?"* The insult worked and Templado reacted, his eyes darting about like lightning. He would not be accused of going back on his word and would prove that he was not like that.

Completely unconcerned, he entered the icy water, taking care where he put his feet. Frédéric guided him and the horse obeyed, trusting his master blindly.

"Stop!" said the photographer with a gesture and Frédéric passed on the instruction to his horse. Templado took the required pose. His neck rounded out, his back tensed up and his thighs hardened. Then he stood completely still, hardly breathing, like a sculpture. Only the mane was in motion, flying up and dancing around the statue.

It was incredible... The horse was free – free to run wherever he wanted to, free to let panic take him and run away, free to take two steps out of the water and graze on the green grass of the opposite bank. Was it because he was obedient that he stayed in position? What was the chemistry between Frédéric and the horse that made it so unthinkable that either should want to lose sight of each other? The trust that bound them was so strong that Templado forgot about the taste of freedom.

Having had some experience with other horses, I naively thought that Templado, who loves to play tricks, would have taken advantage of these exceptional circumstances to turn on his heel and disappear without a second thought. Quite the contrary. He was not at home and not performing in a show. There were no points of reference there for him. He mistrusted this place because it felt very dangerous. So he put all his trust in his companion who, in this place, became his god.

He took poses, one after another, in different places, in different positions. First with his head up and the mane in a certain way, then the opposite: head down, nose touching the water.

"That's OK for me", shouted Hervé from the bridge. The posed part of the shoot was over and Templado could come away from the slippery bank. As an extra precaution, Frédéric put an old green halter rein on him and I witnessed a metamorphosis. In less than a second, Templado changed from a proud lion to a little sheep. His back slouched, his head fell, his thighs relaxed and his eyes lost their glint. Even his mane lost its panache. The machine had been switched off, leaving Templado on hold. I can't help comparing him to a top model who, between sessions, likes to relax in an old bathrobe in her dressing-room. Once the

pressure is off, it's time to get away from it all. But when she leaves the dressing room again, all dressed up to face the camera flashes of the catwalk or the photo studio, she is the star once more, right down to her fingertips.

Perhaps it is a far-fetched comparison, and yet... As soon as the green halter rein came off, a light flickered in the eyes of the white equine supermodel. There he was again, a beautiful star once more and proud to be so.

We left this set and went further along the little valley. We had begun a series of photos that had a few frights in store for us.

In the waters of the Calavon

On either side of the Calavon, two little sandy beaches seemed to be exactly what we wanted. In the middle of the stream was a grassy, marshy island with, in the background, the Roman bridge that crossed the winding Calavon. It was the ideal location for the next scene: a series of photos taken in movement and for which Templado had to play a wild horse splashing about in the lively waters of a river.

We all arrived by the same route but split up to prepare the staging. Estelle bravely waded up to her knees in the cold, cloudy water to get to the other bank. She was followed by Frédéric and Templado who were already used to the water temperature. Hervé would have to get wet for a longer period for he decided to shoot the scene from the river bed, upstream of us. I was the only one to be spared a dip in this rather uninviting river!

On each bank, we put a wire fence along the edge of the bushes, stretching the ends to meet in the water by means of some plastic pickets brought along for the purpose. It was not a complete enclosure and the symbolic white wire made a semi-circle around Templado, so that upstream the horse was free to escape if tempted to do so. But he never took his eyes off Frédéric. More loyal than any dog, he was ready to follow him no matter how eccentric the exploit, even though he probably wondered why his master seemed to have lost his senses and was leading him – figuratively – into deep water. But… in for a penny, in for a pound. After all, things always turned out well with Frédéric so he would trust him as usual and all would be well.

He plunged bravely into the cold water that was so cloudy you couldn't see the bottom. Then, without any hesitation, he galloped across the river and the island to find his master who had preceded him and was waiting on the other bank.

I was stunned by this scene which was repeated again and again for the photographer. My role, which turned out to be superfluous because the star was faultless, was that of an extra. I had to stop Templado going too far if he decided not to stop at the end of the scene, in spite of the white wire of the flimsily-constructed enclosure. But each time Templado ran only to Frédéric, who was also running, and the white wire and I were unnecessary. Each reunion was very intense. Templado simply melted into his master's arms, enveloped him in his mane and put his head on Frédéric's shoulder, whispering his joy of being there with him after each mad dash across the river bed.

"Once more, if possible," Hervé would say. *"No problem,"* Frédéric would answer.

He took the horse's mane and led him calmly back across the muddy little river once again. Templado did it without batting an eyelid, walking nonchalantly as if completely unconcerned. Once on the other side, Estelle would hold him while Frédéric jumped into the water and came back towards me. Estelle had to fight to keep Templado with her for as long as possible, for he was furious at being kept at a distance from his master. Then, with a violent toss of his head, he would almost tip Estelle into the water. Once free of her, he would bound into the river, climb onto the island, step down again into the water and end up by throwing himself on the one who had been so mischievous as to leave him.

Each time we did the scene, the more I was amazed. One rehearsal was all that was needed to set all the action. The first crossing was the most difficult. Templado got a bit annoyed, pawing the ground with anger because he didn't understand the sequence. On the second take, he found his marks and for each of following takes he was completely in character, refining his part each time the sequence was repeated.

Any other horse would have acted in the completely opposite way. He would probably have been hesistant and refused at the first attempt. And even if he had agreed to go into the water, he would have got more and more annoyed at having to do the same apparently senseless sequence over and over again… Templado, however, became calm as soon as he understood what the sequence was about so that, at the end, he went into the water with such self-assurance that I almost thought he was going to gallop right up to me and wink.

Appendices

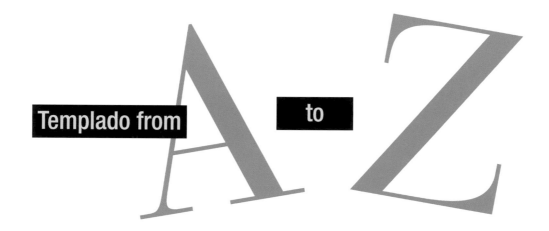

Templado from A to Z

The idea of a glossary devoted to Templado came to me after observing him over a long period. He is so changeable that a whole range of nouns and adjectives comes to mind. Getting the number down to fifty has not been easy but here is a list of words which I hope will complete the image of this horse, and which are indispensable if you want to understand him.

1 Affectionate

This is difficult to believe because he is so discreet and macho about showing what he really feels in his heart. His emotional life is his own business and nobody else's. But he is basically an old softy: a heart of velvet in a body of steel. The sight of Frédéric makes him melt with happiness and he returns Frédéric's caresses by putting his head gently on his shoulder. But he only reserves these favours for Frédéric. I dare you to go into his stall and try to stroke him!

2 Bad-tempered

Although he is not bad-tempered by nature, Templado has found this to be a good way of expressing his determination not to bend to the will of human beings. Ever since he found common ground with Frédéric, he doesn't have fits of anger any more because there is no longer any reason to get himself into such a state. Even so, be careful! It would only take a slight upset to reawaken the wrath that lies dormant inside him.

3 Beautiful

He is indeed beautiful, but only when he wants to be. He is aware of his beauty and uses it to his own advantage. He can be superb one moment and then, the next moment, quite unattractive. He can look like an oil painting one moment and a bad sketch the next. But when he decides to look beautiful, he is truly matchless.

4 Charisma

The charisma that emanates from him is almost unbelievable. The mere flash of his black eyes, or a simple movement, and all the spectators' eyes are riveted on him. Even if Frédéric puts other horses on stage with him, it is always Templado that you look at first. You only notice the others if you make a conscious effort to look away. The other horses also feel this charisma and remain shy and in awe of him. Without any need for force or any malice, he has them at his feet, for he demands their natural respect.

5 Commanding

A natural leader, Templado reigns over his stable companions as if by birth. His appearance too is commanding in that you cannot take your eyes off him, no matter what is going on around him.

6 Excessive

He spends his time going from one extreme to the other and is difficult to follow in his moods. Sometimes you lose him – you don't know how to deal with him – and this amuses him greatly!

7 Exclusive

Only one being is important to him and that is Frédéric. The others just don't count. You can try anything you like, he will look straight through you. You only exist if you are one of those sitting on the crowded bleachers, with thousands of other spectators, ready to give him a standing ovation.

8 Explosive

His outbursts can be quite terrible. You had best avoid them and better still not provoke them. People who have been on the receiving end won't forget them in a hurry. He can also be explosive in performance when he decides to amaze everyone. He brings the whole box of tricks into play: his best paces, his tosses of the head to show off his mane. *"Sometimes, he gets so carried away that I almost lose control. I get the impression that I've taken the pin out of a hand grenade and that it will blow up in my face if I don't get the pin back in just in time."*

9 Expressive

He speaks with his eyes, his nostrils and his ears. You can read his feelings by looking at his head. Never featureless, it expresses everything that Templado would say if he could talk.

10 Faithful

Such is his loyalty that he would throw himself into a river if Frédéric asked him to. His friendship for Frédéric is boundless.

11 Fearful

If you want to give him an injection, you had better send him advanced warning, in writing, at least a week beforehand. For if you don't have his permission, through the proper channels, you will never get past the door of the stall. Even Frédéric dreads these sessions, which unfortunately have to be undergone. *"We try everything before getting out the syringe. But every time there is a scene. And it is then that he goes back to the old panic reactions he used to have when he couldn't control himself."*

12 Free

This is perhaps the adjective that fits him best. Templado always has his own freedom to say no to Frédéric. To prove it to him, during each session of liberty training or work on the long rein, he makes sure Frédéric realises it. If he does something, it is his decision to to it. After that, he will become disciplined. *"He systematically resists the things I ask him to do at the beginning of a session. In this way, he makes it clear that if he plays with me, it's because he wants to."*

13 Gentle

He is deeply, truly gentle. With his character, if he weren't gentle, he would be odious, infernal, uncontrollable and dangerous. Even if he complains on principle, even if he gets Frédéric's back up deliberately, he always ends up by gently complying. And if an importunate visitor comes to greet him in his stall, he will remove him very smartly but without hurting him!

14 Grumpy

He complains for the sake of it. But he is basically patient and there always comes a moment when he stops complaining and throws himself wholeheartedly into playing games with Frédéric. (Has any of this rubbed off on his master, Magali wonders…)

15 Happy

The notion of happiness is so subjective that even humans spend their lives wondering if they are happy or not. It is therefore very risky to say that a horse is happy. As far as Templado is concerned though, one can say without fear of contradiction that he is not unhappy. And if happiness means having friends around you who understand you and whom you love and understand too, then Templado is happy. If happiness also means taking full advantage of life – without the problems of the past, which remain there by way of comparison – then yes, Templado is happy.

16 Helpful

With his years of experience, his gentleness, his ability to be strict, and with his charisma, Templado is the ideal master to initiate youngsters into collective liberty training. So Frédéric always makes him do this job when a new horse joins the group.

17 Humble

When a noble lord like Templado puts one knee on the ground as a demonstration of allegiance, this is moving to the point of being embarrassing. When Templado bows to his audience, one almost wants to say *"Please get up, we are the ones who should be bowing to you."*

18 Hypersensitive

He simply could not be more sensitive. His intelligence and character bear witness to his ever-present hypersensitivity which lies just beneath the surface. It is what distinguishes him from other horse and is both his strength and his weakness.

19 Impressive

He is impressive when he rears up, when he gets angry, when he swells his neck up… One is in awe of him. He loves having this power over others and exercises it unreservedly over those who are less self-assured.

20 Intelligent

How is it that a horse can feel the power he exerts over his companions and over human beings? How is it that a horse can create such close ties with a man? How is it that a horse can understand perfectly what a man is asking him to do when that man is standing so far away? If that is not intelligence, what is?

21 Jealous

He is extremely jealous of Frédéric whom he watches and spies on to see if his friend will dare to deceive him by bestowing his favours on another. But he knows deep down that this will never happen. Frédéric has proved more than once that the feeling is mutual.

22 Joyful

After the sadness and isolation of his early years, Templado is now enjoying life to the full, with good humour, energy and a sense of fun.

23 Khaki

His favourite colour. After he has spent the night lying down in his stall or has stretched out for a nice afternoon nap, Templado wears a grubby khaki garment as a sort of housecoat. It doesn't suit him that well, but it feels so good rolling around in one's bed especially when it's dirty!

24 Light and airy

When he walks with that sweeping gait or trots hardly touching the ground, his neck swollen up and head high, or when his mane and tail swirl about him, he is like a figure from some ancient legend who has come down from heaven to earth just for our delight.

25 Listless

Still waters run deep. If Templado seems calm, taciturn, lethargic and even a bit limp in his stall, don't be deceived by this. He may seem expressionless and listless, but this is all the better to fool you. When he springs into action, you will get the surprise of your life.

26 Lively

Lively is a bit of an understatement to say the least! He shows his energy and vigour in suddenly taking off at top speed, going for a wild gallop, making impromptu half-turns on his hocks… Age has not affected his liveliness at all.

27 Mischievous

He is as full of tricks as an old monkey. He likes to put the blame on his younger brothers for all the mischief he gets up to. He regularly chases after them and tries to bite them. Then he runs back to Frédéric, very sheepishly, head held low as if to say: *"All right, I know it's not nice to do that, but it's not my fault. I was pushed into it."* And, in order to be forgiven, for the next 5 minutes he plays the part of the perfect hard-working, attentive pupil.

28 Nonchalant

He has the studied nonchalance of those who know they are superior beings. Just like a lord of the manor, he has that relaxed yet highly self-assured way of walking.

29 Obedient

The troublemaker becomes as good as gold as soon as he senses danger. When he is on unfamiliar ground, he shows total obedience to Frédéric for he knows that he will guide him properly. He listens to every word, reads his mind and carries out instructions without a murmur, putting all idea of negotiation in the past.

30 Opulent

Whether completely still or galloping at full tilt, Templado conveys the impression to an audience that here is a *bon viveur* in all his voluptuous opulence, fulfilling himself in the art of performance.

31 Performer

He loves playacting. For example, he loves to play the martyr. If Frédéric asks him to piaff, he will put on the sad eyes of the long-suffering victim, but it's all an act. He knows how to do it perfectly and he could even lift his legs higher – if he really wanted to – when asked to do the high-stepping walk of the *pas espagnol*. But he'd rather pretend he doesn't know how to do it. Just for fun.

32 Playful

Playing is what he enjoys most. Like a child who hates doing his homework, he complains when he realises he has to go back to work. Just get out the long rein and look at him. His eyes show the anger and vexation of having to go to work. But let him off the rein with Frédéric and he's another horse entirely, happily off to play and full of good humour. He is going to have fun renegotiating the rules of the game that he has known by heart for years…

33 Possessive

Move over, I'm the most handsome. Move over and I'll show you. Templado will not stand for any of the other horses stepping out of line. Frédéric belongs to him and him alone. If another horse dares to approach him, he pushes him away and bites.

34 Professional

He is a real pro. Acting, modelling, dancing – he can do everything, but he only does it on condition that it's for something worthwhile. Obviously when he's asked to do a few trifling things in his own riding school, that's quite a different matter. A star of his stature does not lower himself to making a fool of himself in his own backyard just to please a couple of country bumpkins!

35 Profitable

Despite the fact that he was returned to the Delgados to be salvaged and that he was seen as a horse who had no future except to be a beautiful ornament for his stall, he is probably the one who has brought the most money to the stables. It all goes to show…

36 Proud

Proud of his mane, proud of his unusual beauty, proud of himself. He has only to raise himself up to his full height and his proud bearing in itself is enough to crush any leadership ambitions other horses around him might have. But above all, he is proud of his privileged relationship with Frédéric. He does his utmost to charm and astound him every day.

37 Quarrelsome

He becomes quarrelsome when he wants to shine for Frédéric and get the others out of the way. But his presence is so powerful that he has no need to start a fight in order to push them aside. They get out of his way and let him pass.

38 Rebellious

This is the adjective that best described him when he arrived at the Delgados' 13 years ago. Since then, Templado has changed a lot. If today he seems perfectly sociable, his rebellious spirit is still there, just under the surface, and it will resurface again if anyone should do anything to conjure up those old demons. Frédéric knows this: *"For years, he was totally unforgiving of me. Nowadays he trusts me enough to tolerate a certain margin of error on my part. But if we have* reached this point of collusion, it is only *because I always take the greatest care not to make mistakes."*

39 Shy

Like all real stars, Templado is very shy offstage. But when he performs he overcomes his anxieties and puts all of his artistic talent on view. *"He will sometimes get really nervous before going on. I feel it during the warm-up in the paddock. He is cold, inattentive and listless. I can't do anything with him. He is wrapped up in his stagefright and his desire to do well. Then, as soon as he goes on to perform, he loses all this anxiety. He comes to me, and listens. Sometimes the change is so radical that I have trouble channelling all his energy the right way."*

40 Silken

When he is not in khaki, when he lets himself be pampered to go out for a grand occasion, his white coat shines and glows like silk and his long mane shimmers like an opera scarf.

41 Stallion

He is a stallion but not yet a stud. One day perhaps Frédéric will announce the birth of Templado Junior. For the moment though, his diary is too full! On a more serious note, Templado has the self-assurance of a stallion and a character of tempered steel that can send shivers up your spine. This is not the sort of person you address in familiar terms, or with a friendly tap on the shoulder. He must be given the respect that his rank demands.

42 Stout-hearted

Templado is a true professional and, one might almost say, a workaholic. He is always up first for a performance, a photo session or a movie stunt and always the last to go to bed backstage for it takes so long to prepare him for the night – it takes a good hour to rebraid his mane. He never complains about the long hours a performer has to work and he would never sign a petition in favour of a shorter working week!

42 Strong

He may not be physically as strong as Hercules but his strength of character is incredible, forged by long years of non-communication and rehabilitation. He spent so long in self-doubt, fighting against himself and his demons for so many years, that he now knows, having finally reached full self-awareness, that he is the best by far.

44 Teasing

His sense of humour and love of making fun of others is beguiling, but so difficult to describe. It has to be seen in action. He will look at Frédéric and in his eyes you can read his thoughts: *"I am taking you for a ride and it makes me laugh to see you going through all these hassles to get me to obey you!"*

45 Temperate

This is the literal translation of his Spanish name but, ironically, it's the only word in this list that doesn't suit him!

46 Trusting

He has blind trust in his friend and would do anything for him. As for the rest of humanity, his past disillusionment has taught him to be mistrustful in the extreme.

47 Uncontested

Like a politician who has gained an uncontested parliamentary seat or a tennis player who has won a championship match by a walk-over, Templado has no equal. In the whole of the stables, there is not one horse who could beat him.

48 Unpredictable

A raging sea or a tranquil millpond? Playful or complaining? Cooperative or rebellious? These are the question that Frédéric asks himself every day when he takes Templado out of his stall. His moods swing so often and so quickly that he can change from calm to uncontrollable in a fraction of a second.

49 White

Before he got his white coat, Templado was grey – a very dark grey that was almost black when he was born. This lightened over the years. His dapples have lost their intensity and are getting whiter all the time. He is not the only horse to have this happen for this phenomenon occurs in all greys.

50 Zealous

Fired up with energy, Templado is a fast and hard worker always ready to please the master... after having negotiated the conditions, of course.

Glossary

Andrade: The Lusitanian breed has been influenced by four main strains of breeding stock: the Andrade, Veiga, Alter Real and Fonte Boa horses. The Andrade and the Veiga are from two highly-reputed private Portuguese stock farms. The Andrade is a large horse that moves beautifully. The Veiga is a racy, stylish, finely-drawn little horse, much used in bull-fighting. The Alter Real comes from the Portuguese Royal Stud Farm and is a bay particularly suited to *haute école* dressage. As for the Fonte Boa horse, it comes from the Coudelaria Nacional, (the State stud farm) and was originally a draught horse for light loads and used for breeding mules. It is now a horse used in sport and often has a grey coat.

Brand: Some traditional breeders like those of the Iberian breeds (Lusitanian and Spanish) brand foals with a logo representing the farm where they were born. All the brands figure in a register and this enables one to tell at a glance where a horse comes from.

Breeding mare: A mare whose main function is to produce foals. Mares carry their foals for 11 months and wean them for between six months and a year.

CN = Coudelaria Nacional: The Portuguese State stud farm which produces one of the four main types of Lusitanian horses. (cf. Andrade)

Crinières d'Or: In France, the Crinières d'Or (Golden Manes) show is considered to be the one that sets the standard for all others. It is held every year in mid-January, during the Cheval Passion event in Avignon.

Gelding: A castrated male horse. (cf. stallion)

Grooming: A horse needs to be groomed daily. This means using the currycomb, brushing him and picking his shoes clean. Furthermore, show horses have to shine from head to foot when they go out, so the time spent on doing this can sometimes be very long.

Jambette: A figure executed when the horse is standing still. It consists in raising the foreleg forwards and upwards as high as possible in a movement that should have breadth and not be done too fast. It is a simple exercise which is a good preparation for the *pas espagnol* (high-stepping walk).

Long rein(s): These reins stretch the whole length of the horse's body and enable the trainer to work on foot, following behind the horse. This is an essential exercise in preparation for harnessing and is also widely used in *haute école* dressage. Long rein work has also become a specific discipline.

Lusitanian: This former Portuguese warhorse that was almost forgotten at one point has been revived for work in bullfights and for *haute école* dressage at which it excels. This rebirth has raised enormous new interest in the horse; a great many amateur riders would like to own one as would professional riders who compete in dressage events. Lusitanians are both docile and gentle but they are also keen, quick to react and brave. They are appreciated for their collected walk, suppleness and natural balance.

The Lusitanian is a baroque style of horse with excellent proportions: a sub-convex head, a powerful neck held erect, a neat body, a short strong back, a slightly sloping croup, slender limbs and small feet. One of its distin-guishing features is its long luxuriant mane.
It used to be grouped together with its Spanish neighbours under the name Andalusian or Iberian, but has had its own stud book since 1966. In 1988, the breed was recognised in France by the Haras Nationaux (National Stud Farm).

Paddock: This is a fairly restricted space large enough for horses to relax and graze in. By extension, paddocks in horse shows are warm-up and relaxation areas for use before the performance. In this case, they are sand and not grass.

Passage: A horse's natural walk: tail up, and head held high, he trots proudly and keeps each foot held up for a moment before placing it down again.
In dressage, the *passage* is a diagonal, suspended trot that is the result of a considerable amount of preparation with horses who are already physically mature and trained. The aim is to make the horse hold each movement as long as possible by increasing the extent of the upward movement.

Piaffer: This *haute école* exercise is a sort of *passage* on the spot, in which the horse goes from one diagonal to the other.

Poste: A dangerous stunt which consists of the rider standing upright on the backs of horses while at a gallop. There may be teams of three, four, six or even more horses. In the case of four horses, they are harnessed in pairs. The rider gets up on the two rear horses and drives the front horses using traces.

Rear (up): When a horse rears, it rises up on its hind legs. It is a natural movement that the horse uses as a means of defence or, in the case of the stallion, as a means of attack. The one used in live performance and in the cinema requires particularly strong back and hock muscles. Therefore, when a young horse is taught to rear, it will take time for him to find his balance and gain enough strength to stay upright.

Roman chariot: For those who have not seen *Ben Hur*, Roman chariots were small, light, military vehicles, designed for maximum speed. They were either drawn by one horse or by a pair. Being very unstable, they were easily knocked over. Chariot races attracted huge crowds who came to see what was in fact a very dangerous sport. Nowadays, you can still see chariots in the movies, driven by stunt riders.

Spike: A turnout of Russian origin in which horses are harnessed abreast of each other.

Stallion: A non-castrated horse. Most males are castrated when young, before the age of three or four, and are then called geldings. Stallions are only kept for reproduction purposes or for competition (with the aim of showing them at their best and selling them as studs). However, in the case of some breeds, notably the Lusitanian or the pure-bred Spanish horse, castration is not systematic as it is considered that geldings have less panache. Handling stallions can be difficult and requires a great deal of experience.

Stud: A non-castrated male used for reproduction.

Dedications

$\mathcal{T}$EMPLADO CAME INTO OUR LIFE by one of those incredible strokes of luck that can change the habits of a lifetime. Little by little we learned from him and took him into our lives. He has the charisma of some of those great masters you meet during your life and is one of those who teaches you that nothing is simple or pre-ordained. He gave us the keys to open the doors of patience and respect and then the dance began. Perfectly in tune, we have played on some of the most wonderful stages in the world, strengthening our friendship in performance.

When I think of him, I relive all those special moments – our games, our fits of temper, our joys and our difficulties. I imagine moments to come, discoveries we will make together and, sometimes, with a lump in my throat, I also think of the moment when we will go our separate ways…

We are delighted that this book has been published and thank all those who have contributed to it. We hope that you will read it with as much pleasure as we have had in recalling so much about the life of this exceptional horse.

Frédéric and Magali

$\mathcal{T}$HIS HORSE DEFIES ALL SUPERLATIVES.
From his earliest years, this well-born son
of Perdigon showed that he was no ordinary horse.
Too much character, too much personality,
too much aggression, too much of everything.
Luckily, Templado's path crossed that of Frédéric
and this formidable stallion has since become,
over time, a most valued partner. And this is how
I saw him under the lights – a magnificent grey
stallion with such beauty, such a mane, such
presence, such closeness to Frédéric,
and such a joy to photograph… Bravo!

Thierry Ségard

$\mathcal{J}$ TOOK PHOTOS OF TEMPLADO as I would
normally photograph people.
I choose the place, the angles and set the tone
and rhythm I want, but I never go
into detail over how the final image
should come out. That leaves my subjects
with the choice of role and of the way
in which they express their personality.
In photographing a horse, I had serious
doubts about my method. Fred was there
to evaluate the risks, reserving the right
to veto anything that might be the least bit
dangerous for his horse, but he was also there
as 'interpreter' between Templado and myself.
Once we had set all this up, Templado
offered me a real feast when I started
taking photos. He revealed the whole range
of his talents, from clown to charmer,
playing for me but also playing with me
in that he would charge at me and sidestep
at the last moment. In short, I simply had
to take what he was giving me.

Hervé Jullian

$\mathcal{T}$emplado isn't just a great beauty,
    he is a great personality.
He can show bad temper
    as much as he can show courage.
You might even say he's a really nasty
    piece of work with a shock of hair.
Like any professional actor,
    he can also be a ham.
The close relationship he has
    with Fred is astounding.
Templado is really someone!

Frédéric Chéhu

SON OF A PRINCE, SON OF A STAR

A star himself was born.

Emerging, veiled, from a dark cocoon

Like a bright cicada in Provence.

Foundering, stumbling, yet ready to live,

Caressing the earth with a hesitant hoof.

Strands of his mane whisked by the wind,

A silvery rain of falling dust

Lifted in clouds by his galloping past.

Such is our childlike dream

Of him.

Pierre and Joëlle Delgado

Photographs

Frédéric Chéhu

9, 13, 15, 17, 19, 20, 24 (Fasto), 25 (Amoroso, Zenete, Bandolero), 26, 31, 39, 42, 43, 44, 45, 46, 50 bottom, 51 bottom, 53, 54, 57, 58, 61, 62, 67, 70, 71, 76 top, 84, 87.

Private collections

38, 60, 69, 88, 89.

Jourdan-Rey

49, 50 top, 51 top left.

Hervé Jullian

64, 65, 72, 75, 76 bottom, 77, 78, 79, 80, 81, 82, 83, 90, 91, 92, 93, 94, 95, 96, 105, back cover.

Juan Moreno

16.

Objectif-Cheval-Media

27.

Anne Fontimpe

32, 33, 34.

Jérôme Rey

51 top right.

Thierry Segard

Cover, 10, 12, 18, 21, 22, 23, 24 (Perdigon, Guisot), 28, 29, 30, 35, 37, 41, 47, 48, 55, 56, 63, 69, 73, 85, 86, 97, 106, 107, 109.